Strategic Intervention Practice Book

Grade 4

Harcourt School Publishers

www.harcourtschool.com

Printed in the United States of America

ISBN 10: 0-15-365526-7
ISBN 13: 978-0-15-365526-5

7 8 9 10 073 17 16 15 14 13 12 11 10 09

Table of Contents

pact	a	pact
queasy	their	gum
foisted	said	past
venture	to	plot
annoyed	his	check
depriving	now	split
	this	task

1. Dave and Jake / made a pact / about Ann.

2. The boys were planning / to eat a snack.

3. Dave was annoyed / when Ann came over / and asked / about their venture.

4. "Check out this cake," / said Jake / to Ann.

5. The boys' task / is to eat / a lot of cake.

6. Jake spit out his gum / and grabbed / a piece of cake.

7. "Are we depriving you / of cake?" / asked Dave.

8. Ann said, / "That cake can't be foisted / on me."

9. Jake looked queasy / when Dave and Ann / split the last piece.

10. The boys' plot / against Ann / is now in the past!

Name _____

Read each sentence. Write D on the blank if it is a declarative sentence. Write I if it is an interrogative sentence. Then fill in the correct end mark for each.

1. _____ Have you ever baked pizza _____

2. _____ Pizza is my favorite food _____

3. _____ What do you like on your pizza _____

4. _____ All pizzas have cheese _____

5. _____ Do you like thin or thick crust better _____

Read each sentence. If it is a complete sentence, write C on the blank. If it is not a complete sentence, rewrite it, adding the missing subject or predicate.

6. _____ With our Scout troop to a big bakery.

   _____

7. _____ A long line of bread loaves.

   _____

8. _____ The smell of the baking bread made my mouth water.

   _____

9. _____ Tasted all the treats on the tour?

   _____

10. _____ Can we go back again next year?

   _____

"The Cake Game" • Practice Book
© Harcourt • Grade 4

Name _____

An author's personal **voice** reveals his or her personality or attitude. The choice of words and unique expressions help readers "hear" personality, attitudes, and point of view. The types and lengths of sentences also give a sense of the writer's voice.

A. Read each passage. Underline the words that show how the writer felt. Then write a sentence that states the writer's feelings.

1. Jake is my best pal. He's more like a brother than a friend. Sometimes he knows what I'm thinking before I do!

_____

2. Dad baked a delicious cake the other day. He's a super baker. When the other kids find out he's baking a pie or cookies, or anything yummy, they all gather in our backyard. I'm the luckiest kid on the block.

_____

B. Read the passage. Then explain how the writer showed that she is disappointed.

   I baked a cake for the class bake sale. I frosted it with special marshmallow frosting and colored sprinkles. "This will be the best cake at the bake sale," I said to Dad. I got on the bus with a huge smile on my face. Then, when I got to school, I put my cake on the table with the other stuff. There sat another cake. It had marshmallow frosting and colored sprinkles. My smile froze on my face. My heart sank. It looked exactly like mine!

_____

_____

_____

C. Now, rewrite the passage above on a separate sheet of paper to express a different feeling about seeing the other cake. Then explain how the words you chose express a different feeling.

Name _____

Circle the letter in front of the sentence that best describes the picture.

1. **A** Matt held on to a strap.

   B Matt made a pact.

   C Matt saw a film.

2. **A** Matt will spend some time at the store.

   B Matt's task is not easy.

   C Matt offered Shannon some gum.

3. **A** Matt has a twin sister.

   B Matt doesn't dread going to the dentist.

   C Matt will check the dentist's teeth.

4. **A** The plot of this thriller has Matt hooked.

   B Matt used to read books in the past, but not now.

   C Matt and Shannon split an apple.

5. **A** Matt's wallet is split down the side.

   B Matt looked at a brick.

   C Matt has no money to spend.

6. **A** Matt got a bee sting on his arm.

   B Matt looks at a crop field.

   C Matt looks across a broad river.

7. **A** Luisa's hat is brand new.

   B Luisa is Matt's twin sister.

   C No one else looks like Matt.

"The Cake Game" • **Practice Book**

Name _____

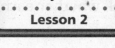

flinched	could	cheese
fluke	for	season
gaped	see	rainbow
glared	she	student
legendary	this	goal
snickering	up	scrape
stunned		
muttered		

1. The Indy 500 / is a legendary / car race.

2. Danica Patrick / is in the race / this season.

3. Danica woke up / at six o'clock / this morning.

4. She could see / a rainbow / in the sky.

5. Danica ate some cheese / and a roll / for breakfast.

6. Danica gaped / at the scrape / on her car.

7. People glared / at the first woman / in the Indy 500.

8. Some were snickering, / while others muttered / that she could not win this race.

9. Stunned, / she flinched / when she saw the crash, / but her goal / was to finish.

10. It was not a fluke / that this new driver / did well in the race.

"Drive Fast!" • Practice Book
© Harcourt • Grade 4

Name _____

Tell whether each sentence is imperative or exclamatory.

1. Clean up your room!   _____

2. Walk the dog, please.   _____

3. We have the best team!   _____

4. I don't want to miss the party!   _____

5. Jessie won first prize!   _____

6. Keep your things in order.   _____

Circle the interjections that you find in the sentences below. Only some sentences have an interjection.

7. Finish your homework.

8. Hey, I heard that you got tickets to the circus.

9. Yes! He scored a touchdown!

10. I can't wait to go to the movies on Saturday!

11. Hooray! We won the first soccer game of the season!

12. Well, I didn't know that.

8

"Drive Fast!" • Practice Book

Name _____

Personal voice reveals the writer's personality. Certain expressions help a writer let his or her personality show. Thoughts, feelings, and opinions reflect the writer's point of view.

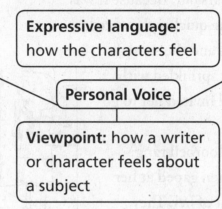

Expressive language: how the characters feel

Vivid language: details that appeal to the five senses

Personal Voice

Figurative language: words that create vivid images

Viewpoint: how a writer or character feels about a subject

A. Read this story beginning. Look for details that show what the characters are like and how they feel.

Althea groaned, and stomped off the field, puffs of dust billowing under her feet. "I couldn't hit the ball if it were six feet wide!" she huffed.

Althea's teammates looked at each other and shook their heads. "Come on," Leah said with a smile. "You're just having a slump. You can do it."

Althea's attitude bothered her teammates, but no one knew what to do.

B. Write a detail from the story that fits into each category.

Vivid Language: _____

Expressive Language: _____

Figurative Language: _____

Viewpoint: _____

C. On a separate sheet of paper, use personal voice to tell what Althea's teammates do and say next.

"Drive Fast!" • Practice Book
© Harcourt • Grade 4

Name _____

Read the story. Circle the words with the long vowels and vowel digraphs.

Today, Susan was nine years old. Because it was Saturday, she woke up late. She quickly showered, and then put on her best dress and the sandals with heels. She ate some toast sprinkled with cheese. Her friend, Sarah, had invited her to go shopping.

Then, unexpectedly, the doorbell rang. Susan went to the door and then gaped at her many friends standing in front of her. They shouted, "Surprise!" and began to sing the birthday song, not a bit out of tune. It was a perfect birthday surprise!

"Surprise!
Happy Birthday!"

Circle and write the word that best completes each sentence.

1. On Saturday, Susan woke up _____.

   nine   late   day

2. She ate some cheese on _____.

   wheat   slice   toast

3. When Susan saw all of her friends on her doorstep, she _____.

   gaped   woke   smiled

4. Her friends could tell it was a big _____.

   fluke   surprise   boast

5. The group sang the notes perfectly in _____.

   tune   goal   shape

6. Susan is now _____ years old.

   ate   nine   five

10

surrender	know	choice
particular	for	brown
sparkling	to	faucet
clusters	went	wooden
sizzle	were	blew
stroll	he	awful
	when	
	that	

1. Did you know / Rob and Don / were good friends?

2. On Don's trip, / he saw brown grass / that was sparkling / with fire.

3. Don made a choice / to go to camp / and eat five hot dogs!

4. Rob stayed home / and went to skip stones / with Cole.

5. Rob and Anna / went for a stroll / to no particular place.

6. When Cole makes jokes, / Rob says, / "Stop! / I surrender!"

7. Don's camp / is so hot / that it sizzles.

8. Don got a drink / from a faucet / beside the wooden hut.

9. When the wind blew, / it made an awful sound / that scared us.

10. Rob's letters to Don / were like / clusters of hope.

"Clusters of Hope" • Practice Book
© Harcourt • Grade 4

Read each set of words. If it is a sentence, write S on the line.
If it is a fragment, rewrite the sentence on the line, adding
the missing subject or predicate.

1. Several small fish.

_____

2. They flashed in the sunlight.

_____

3. Leaped out of the water!

_____

4. Uncle Jake's truck.

_____

5. The truck did not start.

_____

6. Ran to the water and barked at the fish.

_____

7. The dog splashed water on Anna.

_____

8. Anna and her new dog.

_____

9. Rubbed the dog with a towel.

_____

10. They go to the lake every week.

_____

Name _____

Writing Trait:
Word Choice
Lesson 3

Poets and other writers choose vivid words to get their ideas across to their readers as clearly as possible.

Vivid words tell what a writer thinks, feels, and sees.

Vivid words create pictures or images for the reader.

Vivid words make the thoughts and feelings of the poet clear.

A. Read these sentences from the poem. Underline words that show the author's choice of vivid words.

Clusters of grass were sparkling with fire.

Our camp is so hot it sizzles, and we drip!

We will all be in the lot—the whole block will see you!

B. Read the sentences below. Write a vivid word or phrase on each line to help your readers imagine the scene as clearly as possible.

Boy, it's hot! I could just _____.

The sidewalk is hotter than a _____.

There's not a _____ of wind.

The air is as still as a _____.

I saw a dog walk over to the pond and _____.

If this heat wave doesn't end, I might have to _____.

C. Imagine walking outside during your favorite season. On a separate sheet of paper, write one sentence to describe your experience. Choose vivid words to communicate to your readers.

Name _____

Read the story. Circle all the words with the /aw/, /oi/, /o͝o/, /o͞o/, or /ow/ sounds. Remember, these sounds can be spelled in different ways.

Drew and his dad went to an auction. It was in an old wooden barn. There were lots of interesting things to see. The first item Drew saw was an old faucet. He blew the dust away, but he could not read the words on it. The next thing they saw was a big painting of a little girl. It was labeled "The royal daughter of King Henry." Drew set it down. Then he saw an old spoon. It was brown with rust and dirt. He was annoyed when he got some dirt on his shirt. "Dad," he said, "it would be an awful choice to buy some of this stuff! How can they sell it?"

His dad shook his head and took a look at a big table. He picked up a plate. "Now look at this," he said. "This plate has a big crack in it. That's a bad flaw. They won't be able to foist this plate on us, will they?"

Just then a man walked by. He picked up the plate with the crack. He looked at the back of the plate. Then he looked in a small book. "My word," he yelled. "Look at this! This plate is worth $2,000!"

Circle and write the word that best completes each sentence.

1. Drew and his dad went to the _____.

   faucet   auction   flaw

2. The girl in the painting was the _____ of a king.

   auction   faucet   daughter

3. The king and the little girl in the painting were _____.

   awful   royal   annoyed

4. The old spoon was _____ with rust and dirt

   brown   wooden   awful

5. Drew's dad _____ his head.

   shook   look   took

6. The man opened up a small _____.

   look   shook   book

14

accusing	her	screamed
averted	their	moving
craned	were	seemed
cringed	was	returned
fury	the	craned
interrogation	to	watching
solemnly		
stern		

1. Standing on the deck, / Meg and her mother / craned their necks / to see.

2. To Meg, / the wooden dock / seemed very far away.

3. Above her head, / flocks of seagulls / flew and screamed.

4. The next stop / for Meg and her mother / was to pass / the interrogation.

5. Meg stood watching / as a stern man / looked at a sick little boy.

6. Meg cringed / when a man / in the hall yelled, / "Keep moving!"

7. Meg and her mother / averted their eyes / from the stern man.

8. This man / seemed to be accusing Meg / of being sick.

9. When the man returned, / Meg felt / a growing fury.

10. A different person / told them solemnly / that they were free / to go.

"The Best Time" • Practice Book

Name _____

In sentences 1–6, underline the complete subject and circle the simple subject.

1. Meg's boat was near the dock now.

2. An old man was waving to someone on the shore.

3. The man's wife smiled at the big crowd.

4. Three small boys were running around the deck.

5. The whistle on the boat gave a loud toot.

6. The wooden buildings came into view.

Now underline the complete predicate and circle the simple predicate.

7. Meg's boat was near the dock now.

8. An old man was waving to someone on the shore.

9. The man's wife smiled at the big crowd.

10. Three small boys were running around the deck.

11. The whistle on the boat gave a loud toot.

12. The wooden buildings came into view.

"The Best Time" • Practice Book
© Harcourt • Grade 4

Writers choose their words carefully to get their ideas across.
They provide sensory details so that readers see, hear, smell, taste,
or feel what the characters experience. They choose vivid words
to create pictures for the reader. They also use exact words, rather
than general ones, to communicate more precise ideas.

A. Write a few words to describe each feeling below. Choose vivid words.

Example embarrassed: **red as a beet, want to crawl into a hole**

excited: _____

scared: _____

nervous: _____

happy: _____

**B. Read these sentences from "The Best Time." Circle the vivid words that help
communicate the characters' experiences.**

The testing site was made of red bricks. Its big top seemed to rise out of the sea.

The man swelled with fury. His wife sobbed.

She and her mom ran to greet him. There were many tears and smiles.

**C. Imagine taking a long sea trip on a ship like the one Meg and her mother
traveled on. On a separate sheet of paper, write a sentence using vivid words to
describe your experience.**

Name _____

Decoding/Spelling:
Words with
Inflections
-ed and -ing

Lesson 4

Read the story. Then circle the letter of the correct answer to each question below.

Brett and his mom have a home next to the sea. One day Brett was sitting on the dock. Seagulls screamed. A big seal lifted its head out of the water. "What's that I see?" Brett asked. "It's a seal! And it's watching me!" Brett named the seal Casey.

After a week, Casey returned. Brett craned his neck to see the seal. "You visited me last week, Casey. Look! I went shopping," Brett said. "Here you go, Casey." Brett held up a fish. Then he slipped the little fish into the sea. The seal ate the fish. Brett saw that Casey was flapping her flipper.

"You're welcome, Casey!" he said.

1. Where was Brett sitting?

   A   in the sea

   B   on the dock

   C   on a hill

   D   next to a lake

2. What did the seagulls do?

   A   slipped

   B   burned

   C   cracked

   D   screamed

3. What lifted its head from the water?

   A   a fish

   B   a seagull

   C   a seal

   D   a boy

4. Where did Brett get the fish?

   A   He went sailing.

   B   He went shopping.

   C   He went fishing.

   D   He went chopping.

5. What did Casey do last week?

   A   visited Brett

   B   fished for Brett

   C   screamed

   D   fished

6. What was Casey doing with her flipper?

   A   watching it

   B   shopping it

   C   flapping it

   D   scratching it

culinary   a   broad
downcast   look   season
consternation the   daughter
vivid   this   boyhood
extensive   to   returned
serenely
reminiscent
pensive
recruit
commenced

1. His culinary skill / is making / chocolate cake.

2. Ruben was downcast / because his team lost.

3. Mom had a look / of consternation / on her face.

4. Those leaves / all turned vivid colors / last fall.

5. Amanda returned / Ruben's extensive collection / of books.

6. Tucker sat / serenely / on the broad deck.

7. Dad said / this place is reminiscent / of his boyhood home.

8. June was in / a pensive mood / last night.

9. Grandma tried to recruit / her daughter / to help clean up.

10. The family commenced / baking more snacks.

Rewrite each sentence with correct punctuation and interjections on the line that follows. Write **declarative, interrogative, imperative,** or **exclamatory** on the line before the sentence.

1. _____ this was the biggest dinner ever?

_____

2. _____ when will the new school open.

_____

3. _____ Dana drew a picture

_____

4. _____ bring me that toy right now?

_____

5. _____ Hooray. peggy found her purple shirt

_____

6. _____ clean out your locker

_____

7. _____ why is that window broken!

_____

8. _____ kenny ate some cheese pizza

_____

9. _____ My sister found her mitten on the street?

_____

10. _____ That was the most amazing show I ever saw

_____

"The Flan Plan" • **Practice Book**

Name _____

**Rewrite each sentence correctly by adding a complete
subject or a complete predicate. Circle the complete subject and
underline the complete predicate. Then draw a box around
the simple subject and the simple predicate.**

1. The tiny kitten.

   _____

2. Stomped out of the door.

   _____

3. My best friend.

   _____

4. The three brown ponies.

   _____

5. Flew around the tree.

   _____

6. Sets in the evening.

   _____

7. A big red balloon.

   _____

8. Walked to her next class.

   _____

9. Her little sister.

   _____

10. Won the game!

    _____

Read the story. Then circle the letter of the correct answer to each question below.

Andrea looked at the photos in the family album. They showed scenes from Grandpa's boyhood. Andrea knew Grandpa grew up in the country. When he was young, Grandpa split logs to help build a house.

"Your grandpa liked to have fun outdoors, too," Dad commented. "In the warm summer season, he played hide-and-seek in the woods."

"Who is the girl making the snowman in this picture?" Andrea asked.

"That is Grandpa's oldest daughter, your aunt Brenda!" Dad laughed. "She liked to throw snowballs at me!"

"What happened to the house and the woods?" Andrea wondered. "Did someone destroy them?"

"The house is still there," Dad said. "There is a fence around the trees now. A sign says 'Do not tread here. No visitors.'"

"You have many happy memories about Grandpa," Andrea said.

1. What do the pictures show?

   A Grandpa's boyhood

   B a football coach

   C Dad's daughter

   D Andrea kneeling

2. What work did Grandpa do as a boy?

   A Grandpa counted logs.

   B Grandpa grew wheat.

   C Grandpa split logs.

   D Grandpa scooped ice cream.

3. What did Grandpa play?

   A He played tag.

   B He played a flute.

   C Grandpa played baseball.

   D Grandpa played hide-and-seek.

4. What was his daughter doing?

   A building a snowman

   B scraping ice

   C measuring cloth

   D stretching

5. What did Aunt Brenda do to Dad?

   A She obeyed him.

   B She threw snowballs at him.

   C She scared him.

   D She teased him.

6. What happened to the trees?

   A There is a fence around them.

   B They were sold.

   C A fire burned them.

   D They were destroyed.

Name _____

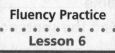

responsible	to	angle
darted	a	ankle
jostling	he	riddle
swerved	said	icicle
attentive	was	sparkle
pounced		jungle
contradicting		tangle
		handle

1. Walt was a responsible lad, / and he faced / a big job.

2. He grabbed the handles / of the big plow / and got started.

3. The tangle of weeds / seemed like a jungle / to Walt.

4. Behind the oxen, / the big plow swerved / from side to side.

5. Walt had to be attentive / to keep the angle of the plow / just right.

6. The oxen / were jostling each other.

7. A shape in the grass / darted past Walt / and pounced on something.

8. Near his ankle, / Walt saw something sparkle / like an icicle.

9. "This is a riddle," / said Walt, / looking at the ground.

10. "If I describe this to Dad, / he will start contradicting me / for sure!"

"Close Call" • Practice Book
© Harcourt • Grade 4

Read the sentences. Then rewrite them as one sentence with a compound subject. Make any needed changes to make the new sentence correct.

1. Walt fed the chickens. Walt's mom fed the chickens.

   _____

2. Walt's father likes farming. Walt's mother likes farming.

   _____

3. The pigs live in the barn. The sheep live in the barn.

   _____

4. The corn is growing well this year. The oats are growing well this year.

   _____

5. Rain is important to farmers. Sunshine is important to farmers.

   _____

Read the sentences. Then rewrite them as one sentence with a compound predicate.

6. The wind blew the tree branches. The wind rattled the windows.

   _____

7. The oxen saw the snake. The oxen started jostling.

   _____

8. Walt looked up. Walt saw a hawk in the sky.

   _____

9. The hawk screeched. The hawk soared above the trees.

   _____

10. Walt's dad pointed at the hawk. Walt's dad said, "Look up there."

   _____

Name _____

Have you heard the word *focus*? It means "to narrow in on one thing and concentrate on it, or to take aim at it." Focused writing also takes aim at one thing—a main idea. Focused writing

- has a main idea.
- includes only those details that support the main idea.
- does not include details that are unrelated to the main idea.
- is easier to read and understand than unfocused writing.

A. Read each group of sentences. Circle the main idea. Draw a line through the sentence that does NOT support the main idea.

1. Walt liked plowing. He felt it was interesting to watch the oxen as they pulled the plow. He liked to see the weeds and tangles vanish as he turned up the rich, dark dirt. His mother did not like plowing and preferred sewing. Walt knew his dad was proud of him, and Walt liked that feeling.

2. Jude the cat was not afraid of anything! He was big and bad! One time, Jude cornered a big rattler. Was Jude scared? I don't think so. Jude was orange and white. He pounced on the rattlesnake—and that was the end of the snake!

B. Read the paragraph below. It is missing a first sentence. Write a first sentence that expresses the main idea of the paragraph.

_____

Plowing with oxen took long hours in the hot sun. Weeding the garden, carrying water, and feeding the animals could be back-breaking work. There was so much work that all family members had to help out. Young children and grandparents each had to do their part on farms of long ago.

C. Imagine you are a young person on a farm like the one Walt lived on. On a separate sheet of paper, write a paragraph describing how you might celebrate a holiday. Be sure to focus your ideas for writing.

Do what the sentences tell you to do.

1. Heather is learning to juggle. Draw three balls on the floor.

2. Heather has a bracelet around her ankle. Draw one there.

3. It's cold outside. Draw an icicle on the window.

4. Heather has several pictures on her wall. One is of a castle. Draw it.

5. Another picture shows a circle of balls. Draw that picture.

6. The third picture is a jungle. Draw it.

7. On Heather's bedside table is a book of fables. Draw the book.

8. Heather likes to play Ping Pong. Draw her Ping Pong paddle lying on her bed.

9. The cords for her radio are in a big tangle. Draw them.

Now circle all the words that have the consonant -le at the end.

inspecting	for	letter
lurked	to	appear
reluctant	her	supper
resounded	then	pizza
rumpled	said	bottom
surge	she	rabbit
taut		
untangled		

1. Grandma and Jay / were inspecting the letter / from her friend.

2. Jay said, / "I like to get e-mail!"

3. Gail tasted the pizza, / but I was reluctant / to try it.

4. Jay's dog lurked/ under the bottom step.

5. Dad untangled the leash, / and then / Jay walked his dog.

6. Mom's voice resounded / through the house / as she called Jay / for supper.

7. The laptop wires / appear to be pulled taut / across the floor.

8. Jay / wrote an e-mail / about his pet rabbit.

9. Grandma's dress was rumpled / from sitting / for a long time.

10. Jay felt / a surge of joy / when Grandma / sent an e-mail.

Name _____

**In each sentence, draw one line under a subject. Draw two
lines under a predicate. Tell whether the sentence is simple or
compound.**

1. Aunt Betty and Uncle John planted new flowers. _____

2. Billy studied for the test, but Jim and Tom played games and sang silly songs.

    _____

3. The circus clown wore a giant hat and drove a tiny car. _____

4. Clay walked forward, and Boots and her kittens swarmed around his ankles.

    _____

Rewrite each sentence correctly.

5. Pam cried and wiped her nose, she was reading a sad book.

    _____

6. Sam plays tag and runs races Brenda jumps rope and swings.

    _____

7. Mr. Miller will lead the Games Club Mrs. Jones will coach the Math Club.

    _____

8. Cathy and Steve played baseball, Joan went to dance class.

    _____

9. Linda cleaned up the toys the children took a nap.

    _____

"You Have Mail!" • Practice Book
© Harcourt • Grade 4

Name _____

Focus your ideas by making sure that each sentence tells about the story's topic. Be sure the story has a beginning, middle, and end.

Story's Topic: All sentences should focus on topic.

Beginning: Introduce characters and setting.
Middle: Tell a series of events.
End: Tell how the story ends.

A. Read the passage. Circle the sentence that tells the story's main idea. Draw a line through the sentence that does not focus on the main idea.

Eric stopped cutting the grass to rest. Eric worked hard on the lawn, for this was his job. He pushed a heavy lawn mower around the yard. This made cutting the grass hard work. But Mr. Mendez was impressed with the job he did. Eric liked to have a cold drink on a hot day.

B. Read the passage. Write a new middle sentence that focuses on the topic.

Amy liked autumn because that meant the leaves were falling. Falling leaves meant she had a job to do. Amy raked leaves for her neighbors to earn money. She grabbed a rake and some garbage bags. When she was finished, she would stack up the bags for pick up.

_____

_____

C. Imagine that you got a job helping a neighbor. On a separate sheet of paper, write a topic sentence that names the job. Then write sentences that focus on the details. Review your sentences to make sure they are all focused on your topic.

29

"You Have Mail!" • Practice Book

Name _____

Read the story. Circle all words with the VCCV pattern that have the same middle consonant.

Dennis and Aunt Cathy took a walk in the park on a warm summer afternoon. They saw children playing soccer. Dennis told his aunt that each player will win a blue ribbon.

"Oh, look at that!" the boy shouted.

Aunt Cathy saw a small animal hop out of a hollow tree trunk. The animal made her think of her soft, fuzzy slipper. But this was a hungry rabbit. They watched as a woman started to offer the animal a big hunk of lettuce. The rabbit ate it right away.

As they were leaving the park, Dennis said, "I hope supper is ready. I am hungry, but I'd like pizza. It's better than lettuce!"

Aunt Cathy smiled, "I agree."

Circle and write the word that best completes each sentence.

1. Dennis and Aunt Cathy walked in the park in the _____.

   fall   summer   winter

2. They saw children playing _____.

   tennis   baseball   soccer

3. The players will win a _____.

   kitten   ribbon   dollar

4. Aunt Cathy saw an animal that looked like her _____.

   mitten   slipper   jacket

5. A woman fed the rabbit some _____.

   lettuce   peppers   pizza

6. Dennis wants to eat _____.

   carrots   lettuce   pizza

"You Have Mail!" • Practice Book
© Harcourt • Grade 4

slick	you	window
nimble	new	perhaps
impressed	looked	jersey
cease	the	mother
exist	to	secret
fierce	he	harvest
	my	winter

1. Hazel thought / her new football jersey / looked slick.

2. Milton's mother / visits him / in Alaska.

3. Milton needs / nimble feet / to walk on the ice.

4. Max thinks Alaska / is cold / in winter.

5. I am impressed / that Hazel owns / this laptop.

6. Will you cease / making that noise / by my window?

7. Niles will buy straw / after the farmers / harvest the wheat.

8. My big secret / is that pigs / exist here.

9. Max thinks the / lion at the zoo / is fierce.

10. Perhaps / Hazel will help Milton / pack his suitcase.

Circle the preposition in each sentence. Underline the prepositional phrase. Draw a triangle around the object of the preposition. Place an X on commas that do not belong.

1. I put my backpack by the front door.

2. Donna jumped over the puddle.

3. Carter bought some ice cream from the store.

4. After the birthday party, Tom hurried home.

5. I will call you, from my house.

6. The five boys on my tennis team, have won ten games.

7. The speedy puppy ran across the huge yard.

8. The TV in my room is broken.

9. The family across the street has four bikes.

10. The wind is blowing through the trees.

11. For my next art class, I will paint a rainbow picture.

12. The clowns, at the circus, were so silly.

"The Pigs, the Wolf, and a Laptop"
• **Practice Book**

It is important that your writing shows **organization**. When you write a story, letter, or e-mail, it should have a **beginning, middle**, and **end**. This makes it easier to read and understand the writing.

A. Read each group of sentences. Decide whether the sentences would be part of the beginning, middle, or end of a story or e-mail.

1. Thank you for looking at these prices. I hope you will think about ordering a laptop.

   beginning   middle   end

2. Max needs to have his own laptop. He will be able to do homework more easily.

   beginning   middle   end

3. Address: Hazel@pigcast.com
   Subject: New laptop

   beginning   middle   end

B. Read the passage. Write whether it belongs in the beginning, middle, or end of an e-mail.

Thank you. I am looking forward to meeting you when I come to Alaska.
Sincerely,
Jim Smith, Laptop Sales

_____

C. Read the passage. Write whether it belongs at the beginning, middle, or end of an e-mail. Then write another sentence that fits with the passage.

A laptop computer can be very helpful if you need to send an e-mail to a friend in Alaska. An e-mail is easy to send and will cost much less than a phone call. There are many kinds of laptops.

_____

_____

"The Pigs, the Wolf, and a Laptop"
• Practice Book
© Harcourt • Grade 4

Name _____

Circle the letter in front of the sentence that best describes the picture.

1. A Linda helped her family harvest the crops.

   B Linda brought her mother some flowers.

   C Linda picked some beans from the garden.

2. A Sandy told her grandma a joke.

   B Sandy talks with Dad about a problem.

   C Sandy hears thunder and hugs her sister.

3. A Billy shared his blanket with his brother.

   B Billy opened his mom's window.

   C Billy loaned a pencil to his cousin.

4. A Perhaps Edward will bring a gift to Aunt Sue.

   B Maybe Edward has a jersey for his brother.

   C Hopefully Edward will buy the poster for Mama.

5. A Jordan gave Grandpa a lucky quarter.

   B Jordan offered a history book to his uncle.

   C Jordan shared a secret with his sister.

6. A Deb helped Mom take out the winter clothes.

   B Deb helped bring food to her dad's company.

   C Deb watched a number of cartoons with her little brother.

7. A Ben's family talks about hunger problems.

   B Ben's family will welcome new families to town.

   C Ben's family donates money every year.

"The Pigs, the Wolf, and a Laptop"
• Practice Book

© Harcourt • Grade 4

unique	a	complete
infest	for	hundred
intervals	me	surprise
delicate	your	exchange
flexible	to	sandwich
bond	the	
inspires	some	
preserve		

1. Your new barn / is unique.

2. Mom will preserve / some pictures / of the old barn.

3. A hundred people / will build / that barn.

4. Mice infest / our warm barn / in winter.

5. Mom helps me / exchange my gifts / after my birthday.

6. Dad will surprise Mom / by hanging pictures / at equal intervals / on this wall.

7. It is a delicate job / to cut a sandwich / for each volunteer.

8. A flexible wood plank / fits easily / in this wall.

9. When I help others, / I feel a bond / with them.

10. The new barn / is complete.

Name _____

Underline a dependent clause. Circle an independent clause. Add a comma if needed. Write _complex_ next to any complex sentence. Do nothing to a phrase.

1. walking on the beach _____

2. when the window is open _____

3. The boy cleared the table when he was done with dinner. _____

4. Because she was cold the girl went into the house. _____

5. The bird flew to the tree. _____

6. hopped to the pond _____

7. brought a ball _____

8. My brother played a game. _____

9. I use a pencil when I do my homework. _____

10. When my teacher reads a book she uses her glasses. _____

Name _____

Ideas need to be organized in a logical way. **Time order**, or sequence, is one way to organize your ideas in writing. When you use time-order words, you help readers understand how the ideas are related.

Organizing Ideas

(Time order is a logical way to show sequence of ideas.)

(Time-order words show how ideas are related.)

(Time-order words, or sequence words, include *first*, *next*, *then*, and *finally*.)

A. Read the sentences. Write them in time order on the lines below.

Next, remove old barn planks. Finally, nail down all of the parts. Then, raise the wall frames. First, get many volunteers to help.

1. _____

2. _____

3. _____

4. _____

B. Read the sentences about making lunch for many people. Write the correct time-order word in front of each sentence.

1. _____, find enough helpers to make the lunches.

2. _____, gather all of the lunch foods.

3. _____, pack the food in large baskets.

4. _____, share lunch with all of the workers.

C. Suppose you had to write a paragraph about directions to make lemonade for many people. On a separate sheet of paper, write sentences in time order. Be sure to use time-order words.

"Raising a Barn" • Practice Book
© Harcourt • Grade 4

Do what the sentences tell you to do.

1. Everyone is in the kitchen. Add some pots and pans on the end of the table.

2. The family is getting ready for a party. Draw a pumpkin pie on the table.

3. Tommy needs some toys to share with his cousins. Draw some monster figures in the basket.

4. Mom has a surprise. Put a fancy cake in front of Mom.

5. Dad had to purchase some drinks. Place a container of milk and a jug of juice in a bag.

6. Although he is a small dog, Ace wants to help. Draw a tiny dog next to the table.

7. Tommy's big brother is hungry. Put a jelly sandwich in his hand.

8. A mattress does not belong in this room. Cross it out.

9. Tommy's granny is not angry about the noise. Circle her big smile.

10. Write a note that says *Thursday*, and put it on the refrigerator.

Now circle all the words that have the VCCCV pattern.

Name _____

comprehend	down	castle
exuberant	our	fable
scan	were	hollow
pliable	we	college
vulnerable	he	problem
nurture		
encircle		
solitary		
lumbers		
mature		

1. Our class went / on a / nature hike.

2. That morning / we were all / feeling exuberant.

3. A quick scan of the trail / showed a / hollow log.

4. A vulnerable tree / had / fallen down / across the path.

5. It was a mature tree, / and a mess / of pliable branches / encircled it.

6. We could not comprehend / the reason it might have fallen.

7. A solitary man /with a walking stick / lumbers by.

8. He tells us / a fable about / a fallen tree.

9. It involved / a problem / with a castle.

10. He told us / at one time / he studied fables / in college.

"Joan's Eagle" • **Practice Book**
© Harcourt • Grade 4

Grammar:
Compound
Subjects and
Predicates, Simple
and Compound
Sentences

Lesson 10

Name _____

Circle the simple subject. Underline the simple predicate.
Then write if the sentence has a *compound subject* or *compound predicate,* or if it is a *compound sentence.*

1. Christy and Michelle went to the amusement park.

   _____

2. Christy wanted to ride the Ferris wheel but chose the roller coaster.

   _____

3. Michelle wanted to see a show, so she bought her ticket early.

   _____

4. For lunch, they ate hamburgers and sipped smoothies.

   _____

5. Michele didn't want to go home, but she didn't have a choice.

   _____

6. Nate and his brother were playing kickball.

   _____

7. Their ball rolled to the girls, and Christy picked it up.

   _____

8. Nate, Pete, and the girls started a new game.

   _____

9. Soon, the children were running, laughing, and playing together.

   _____

10. Some kids rode home, but other kids walked home.

   _____

Name _____

Circle the prepositional phrases. Underline the dependent clauses. Circle the number of the complex sentences.

1. Sarah is a volunteer at the wild animal shelter.

2. She works in the afternoon after she does her homework.

3. On Saturdays, she volunteers for six hours.

4. Throughout the day, she feeds the animals.

5. Although it was raining, she helped out anyway.

6. In one cage, she mopped and scrubbed the floor.

7. Because it was slippery, Sarah was especially careful.

8. Feeding the baby animals is her favorite part of the day.

9. This job that she has done for two years is important to her.

10. She will work at the shelter when she is an adult.

"Joan's Eagle" • Practice Book

© Harcourt • Grade 4

Circle the letter in front of the sentence that best describes the picture.

1. **A** The queen is in her castle.

   B The fable is about a spinning wheel.

   C She will complete the climb.

2. **A** Jimmy's jersey is for soccer.

   B Jimmy needs a smaller jersey.

   C Jimmy's basketball team had a luncheon.

3. **A** My mother told me to clean the garage.

   B The sun is melting an icicle.

   C I don't think I can handle such a big job.

4. **A** Lauren will purchase new shoes.

   B These new boots have silver accents.

   C Next, we are shopping for a mattress.

5. **A** Tom won this soccer trophy.

   B The award is too big for him to handle.

   C Tom's big brother is in college.

6. **A** We arrived early for the luncheon.

   B Today, we will study a new subject.

   C Rachel is telling us a fable.

7. **A** Patrick and his dad will purchase a new ball.

   B The service in this restaurant is good.

   C There is a problem with our car.

predators	a	begin
lure	by	raven
mimic	have	spider
resembles	some	vanish
traits	the	suburb
avoid	to	
obvious	too	
deceptive		

1. I will begin to read / an interesting book / about predators.

2. Some animals / have special traits / that keep them safe.

3. This insect can hide / because it resembles / a stick.

4. Mr. Brown / has a spider / that looks / like a green leaf.

5. A raven / will avoid an enemy / by flying away.

6. A deer hides / in the woods / because its coat color / mimics the shadows.

7. A mother bird / pretends she is hurt / to lure an enemy / away from her babies.

8. Some little animals / will vanish / into small holes.

9. It is obvious / that wild animals / can live / in a suburb, too.

10. A quiet forest / is deceptive / because it seems empty.

Name _____

Rewrite each sentence correctly. Underline the common nouns.

1. The boy found a book about martin luther king at morris library.

   _____

2. I saw mrs smith at the book fair at john f kennedy school.

   _____

3. robert mailed his subscription to 1500 w walrus blvd in new york.

   _____

4. My dad met capt ray becker at the party on friday.

   _____

5. peggy and jennifer stayed at school for dance club with ms baker.

   _____

6. Our class will sing at the stevens point high school football game on saturday night.

   _____

7. My friend, edward p colin, jr, likes to play video games.

   _____

8. My older brother needs to see dr loman for his checkup today.

   _____

9. When I opened my presents, I found a new race car and a box of baseball cards.

   _____

10. The family rode a bus to visit the keeler children's museum at the corner of prince st and n dell hwy.

    _____

Name _____

Use correct punctuation and capital letter **conventions** when you write complex cause-and-effect sentences. When you use these conventions, your writing will be easier to understand.

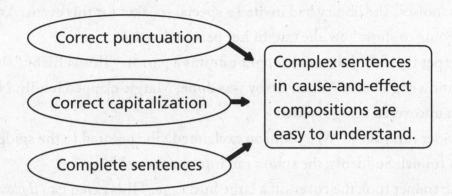

Correct punctuation

Correct capitalization

Complete sentences

Complex sentences in cause-and-effect compositions are easy to understand.

A. Read the sentences. Circle where capital letters are used correctly. Draw a box around periods and commas that are in the correct place. Place an X at the beginning of complete sentences. The first one is done for you.

1X When the weather is very cold, lemmings tunnel under the snow for warmth.

2. Polar bears do not hide behind trees because the land is flat.

3. If the Arctic animals are white, they will blend in with the color of the snow.

4. It lives in a cold place, the musk ox has two thick coats.

B. Read the paragraph. Underline the complex sentence that is complete with correct punctuation and capitalization. Circle the sentence that has errors in conventions.

The walrus stores fat on its body. This fat is called blubber. The walrus stays warm because the blubber blocks the cold. If the walrus swims in the cold arctic water the blubber warms his body.

C. On a separate sheet of paper, write sentences that tell how animals protect themselves or their young. Be sure sentences are complete and use correct conventions.

"Born for Snow" • **Practice Book**
© Harcourt • Grade 4

Read the story. Circle all words with the VCV pattern.

As Margie zipped past the "Please Be Silent in the Library" sign, she smiled. She did not think the library would be quiet today. At the moment, Margie could already hear some strange noises. The library had invited a special speaker for this event. An animal trainer was going to show how she taught her pets to do tricks.

The first pet that Ms. Johnson brought out was a parrot. "This is Bixby," she said. "He can mimic a dog's bark." When Bixby was done, Margie clapped loudly. Next, Ms. Johnson uncovered a large spider.

"This spider can vanish!" Ms. Johnson exclaimed. She pointed to the spider web that looked like a tunnel. Suddenly, the spider ran into the tunnel!

Then the trainer took the cover off a large bird cage. "This raven can fly away but will come back to me." Ms. Johnson claimed. She opened the cage and that is exactly what the raven did. Everyone cheered.

When the show was over, a young boy handed Margie a sheet of paper. It was a list of books about training animals.

Circle and write the word that best completes each sentence.

1. Usually, the library is _____.

   silent   legal   super

2. The library is holding an _____ today.

   moment   event   virus

3. The parrot can _____ a dog.

   mimic   model   manage

4. The spider's trick is to _____.

   relish   visit   vanish

5. The _____ flies around the room.

   rival   rebel   raven

6. Margie gets a list of books on a sheet of _____.

   pilot   paper   petal

"Born for Show" • Practice Book
© Harcourt • Grade 4

constant	around	retell
gradually	could	replace
depths	many	recall
immediate	the	unpleasant
contract	they	unwelcome
revealed	we	nonmetal
eruption		nonprofit

1. The constant rumble / of that train / felt like an earthquake.

2. I heard that unpleasant sound / of our water pipe / eruption.

3. We watched the sun / gradually set / behind the mountain.

4. Those nonmetal toys / will not contract / in the cold.

5. They recall stories / about sea monsters / in the depths / of the sea.

6. The earthquake / was an immediate / and unwelcome event.

7. Research revealed that / many earthquakes happen / around the world.

8. The boys / wished Dad / could retell the story / about that earthquake.

9. We replace the food / and batteries / in our earthquake kit / every year.

10. The nonprofit group / will help families / near the volcano.

Read each pair of sentences. Look at the underlined singular noun in the first sentence. Complete the second sentence with the plural form of the noun.

1. That <u>car</u> went very fast.

   Those _____ went very fast.

2. Carl ate the <u>sandwich</u>.

   Carl ate three _____.

3. Juan read a book about a <u>spy</u>.

   Juan read a book about many _____.

4. Mom packed a <u>peach</u> in my lunch box.

   Mom packed two _____ in my lunch box.

5. I helped peel a <u>potato</u> for dinner.

   I helped peel six _____ for dinner.

6. I hurt my <u>foot</u>.

   I hurt both of my _____.

7. My sister broke a <u>glass</u>.

   My sister broke several _____.

8. Sherry put her <u>tooth</u> under her pillow.

   Sherry put two _____ under her pillow.

9. A <u>bison</u> used to live in this field.

   Several hundred _____ used to live in this field.

10. The boy played his <u>guitar</u> in the band.

    The boys played their _____ in the band.

Name _____

Authors use correct conventions to make their writing easy to understand. Writing conventions include capitalization. Proper nouns are capitalized. Common nouns are not capitalized.

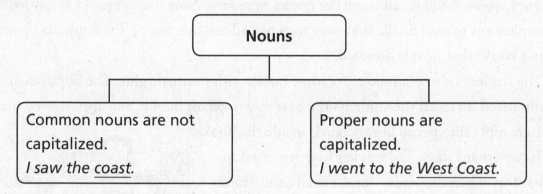

Nouns

Common nouns are not capitalized.
I saw the <u>coast</u>.

Proper nouns are capitalized.
I went to the <u>West Coast</u>.

A. Read each sentence. Circle the common nouns. Underline the proper nouns. The first one is done for you.

1. We know that <u>Earth</u> has a (crust.)

2. An earthquake happens when Earth's plates slip.

3. There have been earthquakes along the West Coast.

4. Some large plates are found near the coasts.

B. Read this passage. Circle the common nouns. Underline the proper nouns.

There are many earthquakes that happen along the West Coast of the United States. Most of them are too small to be felt by people. Some scientists measure these small earthquakes with special tools. The last large earthquake on the West Coast, in Southern California, was in December 2003. There could be another strong earthquake on the West Coast one day, but most earthquakes will be too small to notice.

C. On a separate sheet of paper, use common nouns and proper nouns from above to write two new sentences. Circle the common nouns. Underline the proper nouns. Be sure to capitalize the proper nouns.

Name _____

Read the story. Then circle the letter of the correct answer to each question below.

Some students worked on a new project replacing old books from the library with new ones. Some could recall when the books were new. Now they were old and worn. It was unpleasant to read books that were torn or had missing pages. The students planned to reuse books that people donated.

The students also planned to fix some books with nontoxic glue. The librarian arrived, unannounced, to teach the students the best way to repair books. She also showed them how to reapply the special library labels inside the books.

It took many days. The teacher had promised to retell a story when they were done. Finally, the project was complete. The students settled into some soft, nonmetal chairs and enjoyed the story.

1. What was the project?

   A   to replace library books

   B   to resend e-mail

   C   to unchain the library door

   D   to retell a story

2. How did they get books?

   A   from unwelcome guests

   B   from donated books

   C   from an unused set

   D   from a nonprofit group

3. What did they use to fix the books?

   A   an unpleasant, smelly paste

   B   nonmetal tools

   C   unannounced helpers

   D   nontoxic glue

4. How did the librarian arrive?

   A   The librarian arrived uninvited.

   B   The librarian arrived unwelcome.

   C   The librarian arrived unannounced.

   D   The librarian arrived unfit.

5. What did they do with the labels?

   A   retraced the letters on them

   B   reapplied them to the books

   C   reproduced them on new paper

   D   replaced them on the cover

6. What did the teacher do?

   A   recalled his favorite book

   B   reapplied his rules

   C   restarted the movie

   D   retold a story

treacherous	out	fearless
drudgery	was	usable
plunge	the	horrible
smoldering	something	silliness
altered	looked	excitement
scoffed	could	hopeless
skeptically		
discouraged		

1. Jason gazed / out the window / of the small airplane / with excitement.

2. Being in the plane / helped Jason forget / the drudgery of his chores / at home.

3. A horrible noise / from the wheels / told Jason / something had altered.

4. The pilot, / his mom, / looked skeptically / at the controls.

5. If the landing gear was stuck, / landing the plane / could be treacherous!

6. In a discouraged voice, / Jason asked / if the wheels were still usable.

7. If something on the plane was smoldering, / the plane could plunge / from the sky!

8. To Jason / it seemed as if everything / was hopeless.

9. "This silliness with the wheels / will not keep us / from landing safely," / his mom scoffed.

10. Jason smiled with pride / at his fearless mom.

Name _____

Circle the correct word and write it on the line.

1. Paul and Seth are getting ready for their Scout _____
   camping trip.

   troop's   troops'   troops

2. Their Scout _____ name is Mr. Turner.

   leader's   leaders'   leaders

3. The troop took three _____ to the campsite.

   car's   cars'   cars

4. Many _____ songs filled the air.

   bird's   birds'   birds

5. Paul will never forget the _____ fresh smell.

   forest's   forests'   forests

6. Up in the sky, they heard the _____ loud honking.

   geese's   geeses'   geeses

7. Several _____ ashes were still smoldering.

   campfire's   campfires'   campfires

8. Seth saw some _____ names carved in a stump.

   children's   childrens'   childrens

9. The fall _____ were red, yellow, orange, and brown.

   leave's   leaves'   leaves

10. At the next campsite, the _____ tent blew over in the wind.

    men's   mens'   mens

Name _____

Good writers use different **types of sentences** in their
writing. Varying the types of sentences provides variety
and adds interest. Good writers also use sentences of different
lengths, some short and some long.

Type	Declarative	Interrogative	Imperative	Exclamatory
Purpose	make a statement	ask a question	give an order or make a request	show strong emotion
End Mark	.	?	. or !	!

A. Read the sentence. Circle the sentence type and add the end mark.

1. Start up the plane's motor _____

   declarative   interrogative   imperative   exclamatory

2. She is a good pilot _____

   declarative   interrogative   imperative   exclamatory

3. Have you ever been up in a plane _____

   declarative   interrogative   imperative   exclamatory

4. Look out for that truck on the runway _____

   declarative   interrogative   imperative'   exclamatory

B. Read the sentences below. Combine them to make one longer sentence.

5. The airport is very busy. The airport is very crowded.

   _____

6. Lots of people got off the plane. Their dad got off the plane too.

   _____

7. The children's dad saw them. He waved.

   _____

**C. Imagine soaring in a glider. On a separate sheet of paper, write a variety of
sentences to describe your experience.**

Name _____

Read the story. Circle all the words with the suffixes
-ment, -ness, -ible, -able, **and** *-less.*

Melissa's scouting troop went on a night hike. The darkness was everywhere. The Scouts could not use their flashlights. Even the girl in front of her was almost invisible. But this hike was a requirement for the camping badge.

"This is horrible," Melissa said to her friend Janna. "I just want to be in my comfortable sleeping bag. It's nothing but silliness to wander around in the dark like this! The tree branches are scratching me. And I have a perfectly usable flashlight in my backpack, but I can't use it. This is hopeless!"

Janna's feelings about the hike were different. She was fearless! Her voice was filled with excitement. "What are you blabbing about?" she asked. "Hiking at night is a blast! The darkness is harmless. Just let your eyes get used to the dark. I'd like to hug whoever is responsible for this cool night hike!"

Circle and write the word that best completes each sentence.

1. The night hike took place in _____.

   darkness   silliness   harmless

2. The girl in front of Melissa was almost _____.

   horrible   invisible   comfortable

3. A night hike was a _____ to earn a badge.

   government   excitement   requirement

4. Melissa wanted to be in her _____ sleeping bag.

   comfortable   horrible   invisible

5. Janna was filled with _____ about the night hike.

   requirement   excitement   loneliness

6. Janna said that the darkness was _____.

   harmless   hopeless   silliness

"Mom in Control" • **Practice Book**

© Harcourt • Grade 4

hermit	their	button
fascinated	of	cardigan
occasionally	the	cotton
timid	was	certain
peculiar	to	gallon
drab	her	driven
trembling		
dashed		

1. Kim watched as the skaters / dashed back and forth / on the pond.

2. She and her grandfather / had driven to the pond / to skate.

3. They occasionally went skating / on the pond / at night.

4. In the chilly night air, / Kim was trembling / from the cold.

5. The top button / on Kim's cotton cardigan / had fallen off.

6. Kim was so cold / she could drink / a gallon of hot cocoa.

7. A certain timid husband and wife / standing near the fire / fascinated Kim.

8. It was peculiar / that the husband and wife / wore no coats.

9. Their striped scarves were bright, / not drab like Kim's.

10. Kim wondered / if the man were a hermit.

Name _____

A **pronoun** is a word that takes the place of one or more nouns. A pronoun's **antecedent** is the noun or nouns to which the pronoun refers. In this sentence, *her* is the pronoun and *wife* is its antecedent.

The wife walked down the road, and Kim waved to her.

A pronoun must agree with its antecedent in **number**.

Pronouns can be **singular** or **plural**.

Pronouns can be **masculine** or **feminine**.

Fill in the missing word with the correct pronoun from the word box. You can use each word more than once. Then underline the antecedent of the word you chose.

I	me	my
you	your	
he	his	him
she	her	
we	us	our
they	them	their

1. When the snow started to fall on _____ town, Matt and Jessica had the same idea.

2. Matt knew Jessica's phone number, so he called _____ right away.

3. Matt wanted to tell Jessica _____ great idea!

4. Jessica's mom answered the phone, and Matt spoke to _____.

5. When Matt described his idea to Jessica, _____ was excited.

6. Jessica and Matt decided to build the biggest snowman _____ had ever made.

7. Jessica and Matt started to work on the snowman, but _____ were soon tired.

8. Matt and Jessica needed help from other friends. So they called _____ up.

9. Jessica asked _____ two brothers to help, too.

10. The snowman will be so big, folks will come from all over to see _____.

"Just Down the Road" • Practice Book
© Harcourt • Grade 4

Good writers use different types of sentences in their writing. Varying sentence lengths also provide variety and add interest.

Rosa expected to win the snowman-building contest. She didn't.

Another way to vary your sentences is to use both simple and compound sentences. A simple sentence has one subject and one predicate. A compound sentence has more than one subject and predicate.

subject 1   subject 2
Rosa was sad, but her dad cheered her up.
    predicate 1   predicate 2

A. Read the topic. Then write one sentence of each type about the topic.

Topic: a snowman-building contest

1. Declarative _____
   _____

2. Interrogative _____

3. Imperative _____
   _____

4. Exclamatory _____

B. Rewrite each sentence as stated.

5. Rewrite as two sentences: *Lauren wanted to take figure-skating lessons; however, they were too expensive.*

   _____

   _____

6. Rewrite as one sentence: *Lauren was unhappy. She had wanted to take the lessons.*

   _____

   _____

C. On a separate sheet of paper, write a variety of sentences about a winter activity you like to do.

Circle the letter in front of the sentence that best describes the picture.

1. A The policeman pushed a button.

    B The police car's siren made a loud noise.

    C The police car is on the horizon.

2. A The fountain made the garden feel cooler.

    B We explored the canyon.

    C Many people listen to the sounds of the garden.

3. A Pollen made Maria sneeze.

    B Maria buttoned her cardigan.

    C Maria put on her apron.

4. A The lizard at the zoo looked like an orphan.

    B The lizard at the zoo looked like a chicken.

    C The lizard at the zoo looked like a dragon.

5. A Jack's wrist was swollen where he fell on it.

    B Jack drank almost a gallon of milk.

    C Jack wore an apron while he baked cookies.

6. A They are having chicken for dinner tonight.

    B They are eating dinner in the prison.

    C They have driven to a restaurant for dinner.

7. A The siren is sounding!

    B The score is even!

    C I'm certain the Tigers are ahead!

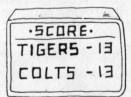

·SCORE·
TIGERS - 13
COLTS - 13

"Just Down the Road" • Practice Book

intrepid	some	event
seasoned	your	retrace
guidance	to	comfortable
undoubtedly	come	requirement
cherish	the	listen
hoist		
delectable		
pristine		
fragile		
privilege		

1. Mrs. Brown, / a seasoned camper, / offered guidance / to the kids.

2. She organized a camping event / for the children.

3. The only requirement / is a desire / to have fun!

4. They will undoubtedly prepare / some delectable meals.

5. Each intrepid camper / should bring / a comfortable sleeping bag.

6. It's a privilege / to come / to this pristine and fragile place.

7. Please listen / to the sounds of nature / all around us.

8. Hoist your backpacks, / and get ready / to leave.

9. To return to our car, / let's retrace our steps.

10. The campers / will cherish forever / their time in the woods.

**Complete each sentence with common and proper nouns.
Circle each proper noun you add.**

1. My _____ lives in _____.

2. Richard likes _____ and _____.

3. Riding on the _____ to _____ was fantastic!

4. Would you like to live in a _____?

5. Shannon is taking a trip to _____.

Complete each sentence by writing the plural form of each underlined word.

6. One man stood on the wall, while three other _____
   waited below.

7. The little calf scampered over to the other _____.

8. _____ make me a little nervous, and that's the
   biggest spider I've ever seen!

9. I love _____, but that tomato is rotten.

10. This canyon is the most beautiful of all the _____ we have
    visited.

"The Camping Club" • Practice Book
© Harcourt • Grade 4

Name _____

Proofread each sentence. Rewrite it correctly.

1. The fires ashes flew high in the air.

   _____

2. Our marshmallows skin's got all burned.

   _____

3. Several owl's hoots kept us all awake.

   _____

4. I'm glad we had a blanket made of sheeps' wool.

   _____

Underline the personal pronoun in each sentence, and circle its antecedent.

5. Elaine picked up the wet hiking boots and set them by the fire.

6. Call Rex and ask him to go on the hike.

7. Mr. and Mrs. Manning like to use hiking sticks when they hike.

8. When Elaine saw the moose, she yelled.

"The Camping Club" • Practice Book
© Harcourt • Grade 4

Read the story. Then circle the letter of the correct answer to each question below.

Andy and his mom checked out a DVD about camping from the library. They were preparing to go on their first camping trip. "Listen to this, Mom," said Andy. "This DVD will show us everything we need to know to be comfortable on our camping trip."

"I'll be there in a moment. Is my cotton sweater on the sofa?" she asked.

"It's here," answered Andy. Just then Andy heard a knock at the door. It was Marcus. He often stopped by unannounced. Mom came in with two bowls of popcorn. When she saw Marcus she said, "Hi, Marcus. Make yourself comfortable."

"I've camped a lot," Marcus said. "Take drinks in nonmetal containers. Metal gives drinks an unpleasant taste."

Andy smiled at his pal. "Marcus, the only requirement for having a fun trip is to follow your advice."

1. What is the DVD about?
   A how horrible camping is
   B how to be fearless while camping
   C how fountains are built
   D how to be comfortable while camping

2. What does Mom want Andy to find for her?
   A her cotton sweater
   B her solar cooker
   C a nonmetal container
   D a quiet moment

3. What does Mom tell Marcus to do?
   A She'll be with him in a moment.
   B Make himself comfortable.
   C He should prepare for an event.
   D She was overcome with loneliness.

4. Why is Andy not surprised when Marcus arrives?
   A Marcus never listens.
   B Marcus is fearless.
   C Marcus is an orphan.
   D Marcus often stopped by unannounced.

5. What advice does Marcus give Andy?
   A Take drinks in nonmetal containers.
   B Take drinks in reused containers.
   C Do not take unpleasant drinks.
   D Find out the camp requirements.

6. What does Andy say is the only requirement?
   A being able to reuse their supplies
   B overcoming their loneliness
   C following Marcus's advice
   D being fearless in the woods

barriers	come	April
forged	something	bottle
hoaxer	been	couple
perfect	they	national
quest	one	normal
tinker	new	puddle
trampled		single

1. Many people have forged / lives / as inventors.

2. They do not let barriers / stop them.

3. George Washington Carver liked / to tinker with plants.

4. When land had been trampled, / Carver gave advice / to farmers.

5. Inventors / on a quest / may get national attention.

6. One might come across / a single puddle / in April.

7. A couple of ideas / for something new / may come to mind.

8. An inventor might try / to perfect / a bottle for storage.

9. He isn't a hoaxer, / but he is very creative.

10. An inventor might make / something crazy / or something / for normal use.

Name _____

Select the pronoun that best completes each sentence.

1. _____ friends came over to play video games.
   Theirs   Their

2. The kids were going to play _____ game.
   my   mine

3. _____ game just came out yesterday.
   His   Theirs

4. _____ scores were the highest.
   Hers   Her

5. We put the game in _____ case.
   its   hers

6. Is Taylor playing against _____?
   himself   themselves

7. Taylor and Tommy will play _____ game.
   theirs   their

8. The best game is _____.
   mine   my

9. When you go home, take _____ with you.
   your   yours

10. Look at _____ score!
    ours   our

"Inventors at Work" • Practice Book

Name _____

Writers of stories use personal **voice** to help show how the characters feel and what characters are like.

Expressive language
Shows how the characters in a story feel.

Vivid Language
Includes colorful words and details that appeal to the five senses.

Personal Voice

Figurative language
Uses words to create vivid pictures in readers' minds.

Viewpoint Shows how a writer or character feels about a subject.

A. Read this passage. Circle the details that reveal how the character feels.

Brenda's cheeks were red-hot. She was frustrated and tired. She thought to herself, "This time it's going to work! This is going to be the best invention the fourth grade has ever seen."

Picking the shiny silver tube off the garage floor, Brenda took a deep breath, smiled, and started again.

B. Choose a detail from the passage that reveals each feeling or trait.

Example   **Vivid language** that is colorful and appeals to the senses:

Picking the shiny silver tube off the garage floor
_____

1. **Expressive words** that show how Brenda feels:

_____

_____

2. **Figurative language** that tells what Brenda looked like:

_____

_____

3. **Viewpoint** that shows how Brenda feels about her experiment:

_____

_____

C. On a separate sheet of paper, continue the story. Use personal voice to show how Brenda finished her invention, and how she felt then.

"Inventors at Work" • Practice Book
© Harcourt • Grade 4

1. This is April. Write her name on her backpack in capital letters.

2. April owns a couple of kittens. Draw them playing in the yard.

3. She watches the arrival of dark rain clouds. Draw them.

4. A gentle rain begins to fall. Show the rain falling.

5. The girl opens an umbrella of a single color. Draw it.

6. There is a puddle in the yard.

7. Draw a flag on a pole. Make it level with the shed roof.

8. A wind vane swivels on the rooftop. Draw it.

Now circle all the words that end in -al, -el, -il, or -le.

"Inventors at Work" • Practice Book

© Harcourt • Grade 4

ancestors	new	director
brilliant	they	tinker
exotic	one	regular
graceful	was	finger
mischievous	could	master
participate	put	labor
	into	dollar

1. Brilliant colors are used / for exotic bird paintings.

2. The art director painted / graceful dancers.

3. My little sister uses a finger / to paint.

4. My new picture is / of a mischievous bunny.

5. Our ancestors were / regular artists / of some talent.

6. They liked to tinker / with paints and brushes.

7. One of our ancestors / was a master craftsman.

8. His labor brought him / a dollar a day.

9. He put his money / into the bank.

10. Then he could buy supplies / and participate / in more artwork.

Name _____

**Underline subject pronouns once. Underline object
pronouns twice. On the line, write whether the pronoun is
plural or singular.**

1. Jennifer will throw the ball to him. _____

2. They brought permission slips in for the field trip. _____

3. We will be going to the museum. _____

4. Another class will be coming with us. _____

5. It should be a lot of fun. _____

Correct the underlined parts of the sentences.

6. I and Margie will sit together. _____

7. Mom told me and Jack that we could play after school.

   _____

8. I and Dad like to shop at the mall. _____

9. Me and my sister read the same book. _____

10. The coach asked to speak with me and Madison.

   _____

"The Artist's Life" • **Practice Book**
© Harcourt • Grade 4

Name _____

Tell students that a writer's tone, or **voice**, gives hints about his or her attitude and opinions. Explain that a writer can also openly describe these characteristics in an autobiography, using the first-person point of view and the pronoun *I*.

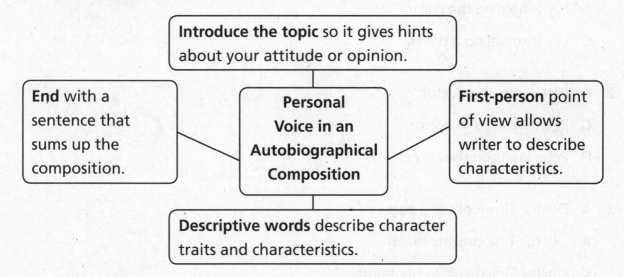

A. Read each sentence. Circle the words that describe the writer's characteristics or reveal attitudes or opinions. The first one is done for you.

1. I flopped on my bed and pushed off the usual pile of dirty clothes.

2. I was so upset about Beth being absent that I couldn't have cared less about the test.

3. I made a face at the dirty smokestacks as we drove by the factory.

B. Underline details that reveal character traits and opinions in this autobiography.

Boy, do I love my painting class. It meets Saturday mornings at 10, but I am up and ready to go long before that. I get up, have breakfast, and get dressed. Then I bounce around the house, impatiently waiting for Mom to tell me it's time to go. In class, I am painting an awesome picture of the planet Varkiel. I use brilliant colors to show the planet's different land features. I don't know how I ever make it through a whole week of school waiting for painting class to come around.

C. On a separate sheet of paper, write a paragraph about something you like to do on Saturdays. Use voice to let your readers know who you are and how you feel about the activity.

69

Circle the letter in front of the sentence that best describes the picture.

1. **A** Lily is going to the cellar.

   B Lily is holding the collar.

   C Lily is spending a dollar.

2. **F** Peter visits the doctor.

   G Peter watches in horror.

   H Peter waits on the corner.

3. **A** Doctor Tina looks at a patient.

   B Doctor Tina eats her lunch.

   C Doctor Tina drives to her home.

4. **F** Yvette speaks with the director.

   G Yvette turns off the power.

   H Yvette jammed her finger.

5. **A** Brendan likes to tinker with trains.

   B Brendan has received an honor.

   C Brendan pulls at his collar.

6. **F** Rex could be in danger.

   G Rex tugs at his collar.

   H Evelyn is Rex's master.

7. **A** Heather likes to tinker with her bike.

   B Heather likes to bake with sugar.

   C Heather is a checker at the market.

bountiful	people	overboard
intentions	there	overactive
inadvertently	they	overpass
resourceful	would	underdeveloped
roused	was	underwater
stature	welcome	subway
vast		
relentless		

1. There are people / in Littleton / who are very resourceful.

2. They went overboard / in planting / bountiful crops.

3. Some people / are overactive / and relentless.

4. Littleton was / an underdeveloped town / from long ago.

5. A visitor would not find / a subway / or overpass / in Littleton.

6. People liked / to swim underwater / and go fishing / in the river.

7. They had / good intentions / and would welcome any visitors.

8. The land / beyond Littleton / was vast and open.

9. People / of a large stature / lived there.

10. They inadvertently / roused everyone / from their sleep / with their noise.

"Troy Bright Saves the Day"
• **Practice Book**
© Harcourt • Grade 4

Name _____

Circle the adjective. Then draw an arrow to the noun it describes.

1. Morgan's ideas are always the best.

2. She is thoughtful.

3. Morgan made several birdfeeders.

4. She hung one in this tree.

5. The birds are happy now.

Write *a, an,* or *the* to complete each sentence.

6. Justin wants _____ new coat. _____ coat he wants is red.

7. He plans to wear it to _____ parade. _____ Thanksgiving Day parade is this week.

8. Justin will get _____ early start. The day of _____ parade will be busy.

9. He plays in _____ school band. The members of _____ band have been practicing for weeks.

10. Justin has _____ oboe. The oboe was _____ gift from his uncle.

"Troy Bright Saves the Day"
• Practice Book
© Harcourt • Grade 4

When you write to persuade, you can focus your ideas by checking that all the details support the main idea.

Clear Main Idea: tells what the writing is about

Write only details that tell something interesting and important about the main idea.

A. Read each paragraph. Circle the sentence that states the main idea. Draw a line through the sentence that does not support the main idea.

1. It's very important to get plenty of sleep each night. If you do, then you will perform better at school. You will feel better, too. I sleep in a bed that's covered with a thick quilt. Go to bed on time each night, and you'll be happier and healthier.

2. Singing and dancing are good for you. Both activities can help you relax and escape from worry. Dancing is a good way to exercise and stay in shape. Some people don't like to dance. Experts say that singing can improve your memory. So come on! Let's sing and dance!

B. For the following paragraph, write one new detail that supports the main idea.

Playing soccer is better than watching TV. You can make a lot of friends by joining a soccer team. Also, it feels really great when your team wins.

_____

_____

C. Now imagine that you want to persuade someone to learn how to swim. On a separate sheet of paper, write two sentences that might persuade them to do so.

"Troy Bright Saves the Day"
• **Practice Book**
© Harcourt • Grade 4

Read the story. Circle the words with the word parts *over-*, *under-*, and *sub-*.

My friends and I have overactive imaginations. We can go overboard with all of our ideas. We love to ride the subway, especially when we go in the underwater tunnel. We make up stories saying we are in a submarine, saving the world. We imagine that we are landing in an underdeveloped place and building a shelter in the underbrush. We will live off the land, and we will survive quite well.

We dream of being tennis players with the best overhand and underhand shots anyone has ever seen. Our names will be in the papers and on the television.

We may go overboard with our stories, but we come back to reality eventually. It is fun to make up stories.

Circle and write the word that best completes each sentence.

1. The narrator and his friends have _____ imaginations.

   overactive   overbite   overhand

2. They love to ride the _____.

   submarine   subway   overpass

3. Sometimes, they pretend to build a shelter in the _____.

   underpass   underbrush   underwater

4. Only a tennis player would have the best _____.

   overdrive   underline   overhand

5. In a _____, they can go exploring underwater.

   subway   underbrush   submarine

6. To other people, their stories may go _____.

   overboard   underwater   overreact

magnificent	their	elk
insisted	these	mouse's
declared	one	children
confidently	was	feet
distressed	were	geese
gloated	they	babies'
anxiously	your	

1. Workers were walking / across that magnificent lawn.

2. Paula insisted / that we hop / on one foot.

3. This elk / stepped confidently / around that mess.

4. One mouse's home / was very neat.

5. These workers declared / that it was a good time / for napping.

6. Ten small children / were very distressed / about the awful mess.

7. I saw many geese / eating grass / from your lawn.

8. Those two babies' feet / seemed mixed up / when they kicked.

9. Paula gloated / when she won / her game.

10. These workers anxiously hoped / that this hot day / would end soon.

"An Awful Mess" • **Practice Book**
© Harcourt • Grade 4

Name _____

Circle and write the word that best completes each sentence.

1. This lawn is _____ than his.

   greener   greenest   green

2. She was the _____ girl at the party.

   more happy   happiest   happier

3. Jack read the _____ book in the library.

   most interesting   interestingest   more interesting

4. Eddie is _____ about the flower than the tree.

   most curious   curiouser   more curious

5. I can jump _____ with this rope than with

   that one.

   best   better   more good

6. Our team is the _____ in our league.

   worse   most bad   worst

7. I am the _____ child in my family.

   older   oldest   most old

8. Vanilla is the _____ ice cream flavor of all.

   best   better   goodest

9. My arm hurts _____ today than yesterday.

   badder   more bad   worse

10. That oak tree is _____ than this elm tree.

    tallest   taller   more tall

76

Authors must focus their ideas when writing a fable. All of the ideas and events should support one focus and lead to resolving the conflict. The characters learn a lesson when the conflict is resolved.

Conflict: Animal characters face a conflict.

Ideas: All ideas are focused so events lead to the conflict resolution.

Main Idea: Character learns a lesson or moral from the conflict.

A. Read each passage. Circle the sentence that tells an idea that is not focused on the conflict. The first one is done for you.

1. "I saw it first! Ha! This nice space is all mine," gloated one worker. "No, I saw it first! It is mine!" each insisted. One worker looked at the flowers in the garden.

2. They saw that he was right. There were ten scrawny feet. Some feet can be large. But their feet were in such a tangle, they could not tell to whom each belonged.

3. "We're in an awful mess," they bawled. "We're stuck."
"Stuck?" asked Paula. "How can that be?"
"Because we can't tell whose feet belong to whom!"
"I am going home now," Paula said.

B. Read this passage. Add another idea that is focused on the conflict.

It was dawn when the first worker woke up. "How awful!" he said. "We slept until dawn! _____"

"Awful, indeed!" each repeated as they woke up. "We'll be late for work if we go home now."

"But we must go home."

C. On a separate sheet of paper, write about a character who does something even though he or she was told not to. Be sure to focus your ideas so the conflict is clear.

Name _____

**Circle the letter in front of the sentence that best describes
the picture.**

1. **A** Kyle caught a fish.

   B Kyle touched the mouse's tail.

   C Kyle saw three elk.

2. **A** Harris picked up the baby's rattle.

   B Harris put away the babies' toys.

   C Harris held the child's hand.

3. **A** Kristin lost the toy sheep.

   B Kristin is afraid of mice.

   C Kristin wondered if all fish have teeth.

4. **A** The class's pet is a frog.

   B The children feed the frog.

   C The other classes' pets are mice and hamsters.

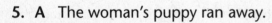

5. **A** The woman's puppy ran away.

   B Those women have three gerbils.

   C The rabbit hid in the woman's bushes.

6. **A** Michelle noticed a moose by the tree.

   B Michelle found a goose's feather.

   C Michelle watched geese swimming in the pond.

7. **A** The horse splashed mud on her jeans.

   B There are little ducks on the baby's shirt.

   C The babies' stuffed animals are soft.

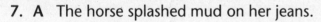

78

"An Awful Mess" • Practice Book

ominous	someone	fish
confound	was	power
miserable	to	gentle
gracious	their	jeans
installed	pulls	national
beams		
monitor		
self-assurance		
exposed		
looming		

1. Danny was miserable / when he didn't catch / any fish.

2. Owen was gracious / and shared his lunch.

3. That didn't help / Danny's self-assurance.

4. It seemed / to confound the problem.

5. Danny beams / when he feels the power / and pulls the line in.

6. The clouds / begin to look ominous / because a storm is looming.

7. They forgot / to monitor / the national weather forecast.

8. The gentle rain dampens / their exposed arms and heads.

9. It's a good thing / someone installed / that outdoor shower.

10. They'll definitely / need to wash / these dirty jeans.

"The Case of the Seashore Crook"
• Practice Book
© Harcourt • Grade 4

Name _____

Underline each incorrect pronoun. Write the correct pronoun on the line.

1. Ally took hers bike to the park. _____

2. Melissa and me were meeting her there. _____

3. We's bringing ours bikes too. _____

4. Mom said, "It a nice day to go there." _____

5. She was bringing Chris and Eddie and there friends.

   _____

6. Them like to play on the jungle gym. _____

7. Theys think they can take care of themselfs. _____

8. Theys needed help climbing them bars. _____

9. Us were happy to help them's. _____

10. Chris and him wanted to learn what they're should do.

    _____

"The Case of the Seashore Crook"
• Practice Book
© Harcourt • Grade 4

Name _____

A. Underline the incorrect adjective or article. Write the correct word on the line.

1. We had a excellent time. _____

2. It was the goodest show I had ever seen. _____

3. Marina was the most prettier actress. _____

4. I think this movie was the more worse I have ever seen. _____

5. Kelly runs more better than anyone else. _____

6. There is several kid who is almost as fast. _____

7. Kelly is going to be famouser when she gets big. _____

8. She always wins the more medals at the meets. _____

9. Coach says if she tries, she will get most faster. _____

10. I would like to be the good runner of all. _____

"The Case of the Seashore Crook"
• Practice Book
© Harcourt • Grade 4

Circle the letter in front of the sentence that best describes
the picture.

1. A We were excited about the baby's arrival.

   B Our dog's collar is loose.

   C My brother and I play checkers.

2. A We hid in the underbrush.

   B There is a gentle rain falling.

   C Our power went out.

3. A Look at all the fish I caught.

   B There isn't a single cloud in the sky.

   C Today is a national holiday.

4. A Be careful not to become overheated.

   B Doctor Dan said I was okay.

   C Our car is on level two.

5. A I am gentle with my bunny.

   B The farmer wears jeans.

   C The sheep are grazing.

6. A Dr. Dan said, "Fish is good to eat."

   B We hid in the underbrush.

   C We threw the small fish overboard.

7. A We like to fish on Saturday.

   B Our power is back on.

   C My fishes' bowl is clean.

"The Case of the Seashore Crook"
• Practice Book

© Harcourt • Grade 4

consisted	friends	assistant
recalls	have	different
snatched	was	engineer
select	here	librarian
intend	into	motorist
prideful	some	confident
	where	electrician

1. The dog / snatched some ham from his dinner / and chewed it.

2. Sue's dad / got a select job / as an engineer.

3. Dad / had a different job / as an assistant electrician.

4. They have been living here long enough / to feel confident / that they will stay.

5. Sue's dad wonders / if a passing motorist / recalls seeing the dog / walk into town.

6. Sue decided / that if she could pick where to live, / she would choose / her town.

7. Sue's dad was prideful / because she took / such good care / of Teddy.

8. Teddy's favorite dinner / consisted of ham, / bread, / and cheese.

9. Sue was friends / with the local librarian.

10. Sue and her dad / intend to make a new home / with Teddy.

Name _____

Underline the verb or verb phrase in each sentence. Circle the helping verbs.

1. Tiger and Snowball play with the string.

2. The cats will hide in the laundry basket.

3. Max chases the cats down the hall.

4. The dog is looking for the cats underneath the chairs.

5. They are peeking at Max from behind the couch.

6. They jump out.

7. Max has been listening for noises.

8. The cats are now running for the stairway.

9. All three animals enjoy this game of chase.

10. The dog and the cats will be sleeping all afternoon.

"My New Dog" • **Practice Book**
© Harcourt • Grade 4

When writing a narrative paragraph, writers use vivid and interesting words to describe the characters, setting, and actions.

Words are specific, not general.

Words make colorful descriptions of the characters and their actions.

Words help readers create pictures of characters and events in their minds.

A. Read the passage below. Follow the directions.

Example   Underline a vivid verb in the first sentence of this paragraph.

Miguel spied the suitcases in the hallway, and his stomach dropped. The smell of freshly baked cinnamon bread floating from the kitchen was another bad sign. His mother always baked cinnamon bread just before announcing that his father was starting another new job. It was her way of letting Miguel know she was sorry that his world was about to turn upside-down again.

1. Circle another vivid verb in the paragraph.

2. Put a box around a colorful description in the second sentence.

3. Underline words in the last sentence that help you form a picture of the events.

B. Read the passage below. Describe the picture that the words form in your mind.

She could hear the jingling of the tags and collar as she opened the door. The knob barely turned before a bouncing, licking, wagging ball of fur knocked her backward onto the front porch.

_____

_____

C. Now imagine what might happen after the girl is greeted by her puppy. Write two more sentences using colorful, specific words to tell what happens next. Use another sheet of paper.

Read the story. Circle all words with the suffixes *-ant*, *-ent*, *-eer*, *-ist*, or *-ian*.

Sara's mother is a musician. She is a pianist. She travels all over the world for her concerts. She likes to have Sara travel with her. Sara has learned many things during these trips. She often gets to be an assistant and help to prepare for the shows. Sara also has time to sightsee. She has learned about how different people live and work. In Japan, Sara met an engineer who designed a building that used a special air conditioner with a liquid coolant. The system was clean and good for the environment. In France, she met a cyclist who competed in a famous bike race. Sara loves to travel. These trips have made her a very confident young lady.

Circle and write the word that best completes each sentence.

1. Sara's mother is a famous _____.

   librarian   activist   musician

2. Sometimes, Sara is an _____ and helps to set up for shows.

   assistant   pianist   activist

3. Sara met an _____ in Japan that designed a special building.

   architect   electrician   engineer

4. The building used a liquid _____ that was safe for the environment.

   coolant   air conditioner   disinfectant

5. Sara also met a _____ who competed in a famous race.

   motorist   cyclist   comedian

6. Her travels have made Sara a very _____ young lady.

   radiant   unhappy   confident

Name _____

burst	into	instead
comforted	said	include
huddle	was	outbreak
journey	already	downfall
opportunities	friendship	update
recognizes	to	up-front
	the	uphill

1. Eva said / that their new opportunities / would include Dad's new job.

2. Instead of being glad to go, / Marta burst into tears / while packing.

3. Eva tries / to update her diary often / during the journey.

4. Eva's father / was driving uphill / when he pulled over / to put on snow chains.

5. The girls / huddle together / in the cold.

6. Eva would not let her doubts / be her downfall.

7. She recognizes / that she will have / new opportunities / for friendship, too.

8. A silly license plate game / creates an outbreak of giggling / on the third day.

9. The family was comforted / knowing that they / already had relatives / in Cleveland.

10. Isabel / was up-front with Marta / about her / lack of patience.

Name _____

Read each sentence. Underline the verb or verbs. Write
action or *linking* **to tell what kind of verb is used in the sentence.**

1. Emily is my red standard poodle. _____

2. Red poodles are rare. _____

3. Emily wags her tail as we are driving to the dog park. _____

4. Emily leaps through the gate of the park. _____

5. Emily grabs a tennis ball. _____

6. All of the dogs race after the ball. _____

Read each sentence. Write *linking verb* or *helping verb* to identify the underlined word.

7. My mom and I are dog trainers. _____

8. My mom is taking the dogs to the park. _____

9. My dog and I are racing across the field. _____

10. My dog is very happy. _____

88

"Dear Diary" • Practice Book

Name _____

Good writers choose precise words that tell exactly what happened and how they felt about what happened. One way they do this is by using vivid, descriptive words.

Vivid words create pictures or images for the reader.

Vivid words tell what a writer thinks, feels, and sees.

Vivid words make the thoughts and feelings of the writer clear.

A. Read the sentences below. Underline the vivid words.

Example   It was <u>drifting</u> and <u>swirling</u> all around.

It was funny how her eyes widened as she peered out at the snow.

Isabel had wild, curly hair.

B. Read the sentences below. Underline the vivid, descriptive words.

Karen lay on her back in the snow and looked up at the sky. The clouds were flat gray, cool steel, and bright silver in places. She squinted against the reflected glare as the sun tried to burn through the clouds. Then the calm was swept away by a stiff breeze followed by a gust of wind and another, second gust that made the nearby forest howl as it pushed through the bare branches. The holes in the clouds closed and the first delicate flakes of a new snowstorm appeared above her, twirling, sailing, sifting down.

C. Imagine walking outside during your favorite season. On a separate sheet of paper, write sentences with vivid words to describe what you see, hear, feel, or smell.

_____

_____

Name _____

Circle the letter in front of the sentence that best describes the picture.

1. **A** Baseball is an outdoor game.

    B Will they wear that outfit dancing?

    C That hat is kind of outdated.

2. **A** She inferred it would soon rain.

    B She liked the infield positions.

    C The infant was too young to play.

3. **A** Since he was too young to play, they let him update the scoreboard.

    B He wanted to upload the score to the Internet.

    C The score inspired an uprising.

4. **A** The count did not include the team members.

    B Their hot dogs were infamous.

    C He wished she wore her small hat instead.

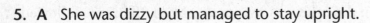

5. **A** She was dizzy but managed to stay upright.

    B She hit the ball upward toward the sky.

    C The player caught the ball in the outfield.

6. **A** The weather outlook had been good.

    B We searched the crowd for outlaws.

    C She caught the ball in the outfield.

7. **A** Mom said they could play downstairs.

    B They preferred to run downhill.

    C A sudden downpour ended the game.

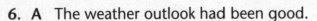
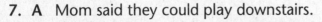

"Dear Diary" • Practice Book

© Harcourt • Grade 4

fidget	about	civilization
forlornly	what	environmental
noble	someone	declaration
pathetic	looked	admiration
resolved	enough	association
scrounging		decoration
stingy		rendition
suspicion		

1. Phil had resolved / to take the bus to civilization / to help his nephew.

2. Phil looked forlornly around him / when he learned / that the environmental hazards of the city / included a cat.

3. Phil had a suspicion / that the cat might eat him.

4. As the cat came closer, / Phil gave a pathetic / little squeak.

5. The cat / ignored Phil's declaration of fear /and asked kindly, / "What brings you / to the city?"

6. The more Phil got to know Ralph, / the more his admiration grew / for the noble cat.

7. Phil's association with Ralph / earned him a cracker / that the cat had found / while scrounging.

8. Someone had told Ralph / about an elephant / that was a park decoration.

9. Ralph gave a talented rendition / of a familiar song.

10. Phil had learned enough about Ralph / to know that the cat / could never be stingy.

Grammar: Present-
Tense Verbs;
Subject-Verb
Agreement
. . . .
Lesson 23

Name _____

Read each sentence. Circle the correct word, and write it in the blank.

1. Manuel _____ radio-controlled cars.
   race   races

2. Every Saturday his father _____ him to the hobby shop.
   take   takes

3. All the racers _____ up their cars on tables they call "pits."
   set   sets

4. The cars _____ on six-cell battery packs.
   run   runs

5. Manuel's car _____ blue with red and yellow flames.
   is   are

6. Manuel _____ his car at the start line.
   place   places

7. The announcer _____ the timing equipment.
   watch   watches

8. The announcer _____ the race with a buzzer.
   start   starts

9. Manuel's father _____ in the middle of the track and helps the
   cars that crash.
   stand   stands

10. Manuel and his father _____ having a lot of fun.
    is   are

When you write, it is important to use the correct
conventions of writing.

Correct grammar helps the reader understand your meaning.	Correct spelling makes it clear what you mean to say.
Correct punctuation helps the reader see where sentences or phrases begin and end.	Correct capitalization helps the reader tell the difference between common nouns and proper nouns.

A. Rewrite the sentence correctly. Use the clue word to guide you in finding the kind of mistake.

1. *Grammar:* We was sure the store would still be open.

_____

2. *Spelling:* The bazaar patterns on the shirt made it unappealing to Casey.

_____

3. *Punctuation:* I walked home with Natalie which was okay with my mother.

_____

4. *Capitalization:* We took a drive up little creek road.

_____

B. Use proofreading marks to fix the paragraph. There is one error each in grammar, spelling, punctuation, and capitalization.

Jenny is trying to teach kate how to double-jump. She show Kate how two listen for the rhythm of the ropes as they hit the ground. She shows Kate how to find the space between the ropes and jump in

C. On your own paper, rewrite the paragraph in Part B correctly.

Albert Einstein

Do what the sentences tell you to do.

1. The professor has great admiration for Albert Einstein. Draw Dr. Einstein's face in his frame.

2. The professor's hobby is aviation. Draw some model planes on top of the bookshelf.

3. For disposal of his trash, draw a wastebasket near the professor.

4. Draw some facial hair on the professor.

5. He has quite a few student compositions to grade. Draw the papers on his desk.

6. The professor is a fan of the Declaration of Independence. Draw a copy in the frame.

7. One recent addition to the office is a large potted palm tree. Draw it.

8. Draw an open window on the wall to let in environmental noise.

9. Draw decorations of stars on the walls.

10. He belongs to the Science Professors Association. Draw an SPA mug.

"Phil in the City" • **Practice Book**
© Harcourt • Grade 4

advantage	have	effortlessly
extract	through	playfully
remarkable	these	joyfully
stealthy	live	blissfully
suitable	some	respectfully
withstand	they	carefully
	their	
	where	

1. The stealthy snake / slid effortlessly / through the branches / of the mangrove tree.

2. These remarkable trees / live in salt water / instead of soil.

3. Colorful fish swim playfully / around the roots / under the water.

4. Some birds / take advantage of the tree / as a place to rest / and sing joyfully.

5. Today, / the air is blissfully calm, / but mangrove trees can withstand / heavy winds.

6. Mangrove tree seeds / have an unusual way / of growing.

7. They stay attached / and grow in the air / while they extract food / from the mother tree.

8. When the young trees are big enough, / they drop into the water / in search of a suitable place / to grow on their own.

9. Treat mangrove trees respectfully / because they help protect the land / around us.

10. Carefully choosing where to build / new homes and roads / will also help / protect the trees.

"Where Land and Sea Meet"
• Practice Book
© Harcourt • Grade 4

Name _____

Read each sentence. Circle the verb or verb phrase. Write
***past*, *present*, or *future* to identify the tense of the verb. If there**
is an error in subject-verb agreement, rewrite the sentence
correctly on the line below. The first one is done for you.

1. Jake (skated) quickly across the ice. _____ **past tense** _____

   _____

2. Sergio walk his dog through the park now. _____

   _____

3. Helen will go to the dentist tomorrow. _____

   _____

4. Linh hopped up on the stool. _____

   _____

5. The cat jumped onto her lap playfully. _____

   _____

6. Mom talks with Grandpa every day. _____

   _____

7. Jill sing all the words to the song. _____

   _____

8. Raul spotted the missing bicycle. _____

   _____

9. We will read the whole book by Friday. _____

   _____

10. My brother answered the phone first. _____

    _____

"Where Land and Sea Meet"
• Practice Book
© Harcourt • Grade 4

When you write, it is important to use the correct **conventions** of writing. Using correct grammar, spelling, punctuation, and capitalization helps the reader better understand your writing.

A. Rewrite each sentence correctly. Use the clue word at the beginning to find the mistake.

1. *Grammar:* Mangrove trees lives where the land meets the sea.

   _____

2. *Spelling:* Each tree makes plenty of seads.

   _____

3. *Punctuation:* The seedling may drift away to a new place

   _____

4. *Capitalization:* Mangroves grow in texas, louisiana, and florida.

   _____

B. Use proofreading marks to fix the paragraph. There are seven errors in all.

There is many different kinds of mangrove trees. In the united states there are two main types of mangrove trees. There is red mangrove trees, which turn the water around their roots red. They only grows to about nine meters (thirty feet) tall. There are also black mangrove trees, which are twice as tall as red mangroves They produces nectar favored by honeybees.

C. Now it's your turn to check conventions in your own writing. On a separate sheet of paper, write two or three sentences describing a place you know well. Then correct any errors in writing conventions.

"Where Land and Sea Meet"
• **Practice Book**
© Harcourt • Grade 4

Read the passage. Circle all words with more than one suffix.

The air is still damp and cold, but the sky is meaningfully a
lighter blue along the horizon. A male bird is singing boastfully in the dark. As people
in the valley below continue to sleep blissfully, the sun effortlessly spreads additional
rays of light. Other birds wake and sing joyfully to each other as they go about their
morning chores.

A young bear comes up the hill, playfully rolling in
the grass before guiltlessly gobbling down berries from the
bushes. A skunk comes out from under one bush, and the
bear respectfully steers clear.

Circle and write the word that best completes each sentence.

1. Sunrise and sunset go on _____.

   playfully   boastfully   endlessly

2. As the sun rises, the sky is _____ illuminated.

   colorfully   educational   truthfully

3. The people in the valley below are _____ sleeping.

   colorfully   blissfully   playfully

4. All of the birds sing _____ to each other.

   meaningfully   colorfully   joyfully

5. A young bear _____ rolls in the grass.

   additional   playfully   childishness

6. The bear _____ avoids the skunk.

   boastfully   carefully   endlessly

"Where Land and Sea Meet"
• Practice Book
© Harcourt • Grade 4

aspects	beautiful	confident
destinations	groups	decorations
expectantly	you	outdated
festive	do	effortlessly
gorgeous	there	truthfully
misfortune	some	carefully
ornate	come	addition
reconstruct	who	
symbolize		
vigorously		

1. There are many different aspects / of a county fair.

2. You can choose / from destinations / such as the animal exhibits / or carnival rides.

3. Many of the exhibits / are judged, / and the confident entrants / wait expectantly / to hear who won.

4. Groups enjoy / the addition of festive decorations / at the county fair.

5. Truthfully, / gorgeous weather can contribute / to big crowds.

6. Lots of rain / can be a real misfortune / to the fair, / as fewer people / will attend.

7. You can find lots of things / for sale, / such as ornate saddles / for horses.

8. Some people carefully reconstruct / life in the past / for exhibits.

9. The outdated ways of making things / win the admiration / of those to whom they symbolize / a simpler life.

10. An evening rock concert / brings us vigorously and effortlessly / back to the present.

Name _____

Underline the verb or verb phrases. Write the correct verb or verb phrase on the line.

1. Esther had always want a puppy. _____

2. Lukas was watch a soccer game yesterday. _____

3. Shayla and Brittney is trying out for the team tomorrow.

   _____

4. Ramon is fly to his grandparents' home for the holiday.

   _____

5. Emilio runned two miles every morning. _____

6. Dominique is learn gymnastics on Saturdays. _____

7. Quentin will decides what to do when he gets there.

   _____

8. We always fills the suitcases too full of clothing. _____

Name _____

Circle the mistake in each sentence. Write it correctly.

1. Yesterday, Weston celebrate his birthday. _____

2. A few hours ago, he arrives with a new yo-yo. _____

3. Skylar will shows him how to use it. _____

4. Right now, Weston are happy just to show it to all of us. _____

5. Sasha enter the gymnastic competition last week. _____

6. We all wants to see her win today. _____

7. We is sitting in the front row so she will know we are here.

   _____

8. Sasha will competes in the uneven bars first. _____

9. Marisol and Jose visit their grandfather in Venezuela last month.

   _____

10. Today, he arrive to see their home in the United States. _____

11. Marisol and Jose picks him up at the airport. _____

12. Tomorrow, we is taking him to the city for a tour. _____

Name _____

Circle the letter in front of the sentence that best describes the picture.

1. **A** The school had an electrician put in new lights.

   B The comedian entertained us all on the field.

   C The librarian found us books about baseball.

2. **A** The admiral was respected by everyone.

   B We studied environmental changes in our neighborhood.

   C We said an emotional good-bye to Mrs. Parks.

3. **A** She answered her father truthfully.

   B On her new bike, she ascended the hill almost effortlessly.

   C He said he wanted to be more than a typist when he grew up.

4. **A** The problem might have been our inexact measurements.

   B We were each interested in different aspects of the soup.

   C We laughed so hard our abdominal muscles hurt.

5. **A** We had the misfortune of being soaked by the whale.

   B We couldn't easily choose from among the destinations.

   C The class waited expectantly for the show to begin.

6. **A** The old house had ornate iron railings.

   B The old house lacked decorations.

   C They rode carefully past the new construction.

7. **A** John wanted to sit up front, but Jake wanted to sit in the back.

   B John and Jake hoped to be engineers someday.

   C Their lack of money would prove to be the boys' downfall.

"Monterey County Fair" • Practice Book

© Harcourt • Grade 4

contraption	could	scene
roamed	once	climbed
massive	their	exhibit
submerged	these	often
elegant	they	doubt
obstacles	were	unknown
complicated		
eerie		

1. There is no doubt / that mammoths were / massive animals.

2. They roamed Earth / during the Ice Age.

3. Mammoths could use / their elegant trunks / to feed.

4. These animals / used their trunks / to get through obstacles, / too.

5. Mammoths were / once unknown / to modern humans.

6. Then workers / came across / an eerie scene.

7. Workers climbed / onto a hill / and found many bones.

8. At one time, the animal remains / were submerged / in water and mud.

9. It was a / complicated process, / but workers also used / contraptions to find bones.

10. People often come / to Hot Springs / to see the mammoth exhibit.

Name _____

Change the irregular verb in the parentheses to the past tense form that completes each sentence. Write the word on the line. The chart will help you.

SOME IRREGULAR VERBS

Verb	Present	Past	Past with Helping Verb (have, has, had)
break	break, breaks	broke	broken
build	build, builds	built	built
go	go, goes	went	gone
know	know, knows	knew	known
swim	swim, swims	swam	swum
write	write, writes	wrote	written

1. Matt _____ with me to the park. (go)

2. I have _____ a castle made of sand. (build)

3. Cameron had _____ that her mom was coming. (know)

4. Diane has _____ three book reports this month. (write)

5. Jack _____ at the pool for an hour. (swim)

6. I have _____ to that store before. (go)

7. I _____ my name in the front of my notebook. (write)

8. John _____ his leg yesterday. (break)

9. The dog _____ how to get over the fence. (know)

10. My sister has _____ her pencil. (break)

"Rough and Tough Enough"
• Practice Book
© Harcourt • Grade 4

Writers use a variety of sentence types and lengths.

Sentence Types	Sentence Lengths
• Use simple, compound, and complex sentences to make your writing more effective. • Combine simple sentences into compound sentences using *for*, *and*, *nor*, *but*, *or*, or *yet*. • Use words such as *because*, *since*, *after*, *although*, and *when* to make complex sentences.	• Use short sentences and long sentences to keep writing interesting. • Combine short sentences by adding words from one sentence to another sentence. • Combine short sentences using a comma and words such as *and*, *but*, or *or*.

A. Read the sentences below. Circle the sentence type that best describes it.

Example Mammoths were massive!

(simple)   compound   complex

1. Mammoths were rough and tough animals.

simple   compound   complex

2. Give me the bones, and I can take them to the museum.

simple   compound   complex

3. Juan and Maria went to the museum after they finished studying.

simple   compound   complex

B. Read the short sentences below. Combine them into a long sentence.

Chase enjoyed going to the museum. He loved being able to see the artifacts.

_____

_____

C. Now imagine that you are going to a museum to see the mammoth's bones. On another sheet of paper, write three sentences of varying types and lengths that describe what you see in the museum and how you feel.

"Rough and Tough Enough"
• Practice Book
© Harcourt • Grade 4

Do what the sentences tell you to do.

1. This is an island scene. Draw a palm tree.

2. It is often sunny on the island. Draw a sun.

3. Look, the folks are hot! Draw a hat on each person.

4. Walker hurt his thumb. Give him a bandage.

5. The woman is drinking lemonade. Draw her glass half full of lemonade.

6. The man is swatting away a gnat. Draw the gnat.

7. The teenager likes to listen to music. Draw headphones on her ears.

8. Walker wants to play in the water. Draw a water toy beside him.

9. The lifeguard needs to climb off her lifeguard chair. Add a ladder.

Now, circle all the words that have silent letters.

"Rough and Tough Enough"
• Practice Book

© Harcourt • Grade 4

ancient	are	photograph
cascading	come	specific
distant	some	spectator
embedded	the	visible
eroding	to	visitor
glistens	where	visor
sentries		
weary		

1. The visitor watches / as the water glistens / in the morning light.

2. The photograph shows / the water cascading / along its path.

3. The distant river is visible / to the birds.

4. The ancient river flows / through ten states.

5. Some people sit / like sentries / while they are fishing / in the river.

6. The weary spectator takes off his visor / as he sits down.

7. Alligators can be found / embedded / in the mud and rocks.

8. The land of the delta / is always eroding.

9. There are no specific places / where the river ends / or the sea begins.

10. Many people come / to see / the mighty Mississippi River.

"Along the Mighty Mississippi"
• Practice Book

Grammar:
Contractions,
Possessive
Pronouns, and
Other Easily
Confused Words
• • • • • • • • • • •
Lesson 27

Circle and write the correct word to complete each sentence.

1. Do you know _____ jersey this is?

   who's   whose   won't

2. I think _____ jersey is in the drawer.

   you're   you   your

3. Hunter _____ be able to go to the game today.

   won't   whose   don't

4. _____ throat was sore yesterday.

   His   He's   He

5. _____ going to take him to the doctor?

   Whose   His   Who's

6. We have to go _____ for our game.

   there   their   they're

7. I _____ wait until we play the Braves.

   don't   can't   won't

8. _____ going to have to get a seat on the bleachers early.

   Your   You   You're

9. _____ expected to win the game.

   There   Their   They're

10. Do you know _____ banner this is?

    who's   whose   whom

"Along the Mighty Mississippi"
• Practice Book
© Harcourt • Grade 4

When writing explanatory text, writers should use a variety
of sentence lengths and types. By varying among simple,
compound, and complex sentences, writers make a composition
more interesting. At the same time, writers are careful to correct
run-on sentences and comma splices.

| Combine some short, related sentences. | ← Effective sentences keep the reader's interest. → | Use simple, compound, and complex sentences. |

**A. Read the sentences below. Write *simple*, *compound*, or *complex* to identify the
type of sentence.**

> **Example** The Mississippi River flows through ten states. __simple__

1. The Mississippi River serves as a map for birds because they can follow it to reach

   warmer places. _____

2. The river has about 250 kinds of fish. _____

3. The river is a useful border, and it serves as a "drainpipe" for the country's extra

   water. _____

B. Read the sentences below. Combine them into one longer sentence.

4. Dylan went fishing. His dad caught three fish. _____

   _____

5. Bass live in the river. Pike live in the river. Catfish live there, too. _____

   _____

6. We packed our things and left. It had started to rain. _____

   _____

**C. Now imagine that you are visiting the Mississippi River. On your own paper,
write a complex sentence describing what you would like to do or see.**

"Along the Mighty Mississippi"
• **Practice Book**
© Harcourt • Grade 4

Circle the letter in front of the sentence that best describes the picture.

1. A Paula takes a photograph of the ocean.

   B Paula is a spectator of the show.

   C Paula is a visitor here every year.

2. A A visitor gets into the picture.

   B A person tries to get her autograph.

   C The trash is visible.

3. A Paula's telephone rings.

   B Paula needs to wear her visor.

   C Paula can hear the television.

4. A Paula inspects the camera for dirt.

   B Paula instructs the boy on how to take a picture.

   C The little boy constructs a sand castle.

5. A The little boy looks for a specific shell.

   B The little boy makes a spectacle of himself.

   C The little boy builds another sand structure.

6. A Paula takes a photograph of the boy and his shell.

   B The inspector looks at Paula's camera.

   C The little boy wants to watch television.

7. A Paula receives a telegraph from her brother.

   B The little boy learns phonics at school.

   C There is a spectacular view of the ocean from this dock.

"Along the Mighty Mississippi"
• Practice Book

© Harcourt • Grade 4

Name _____

behemoth	everyone	our
colossal	have	plain
cordially	lived	seem
fanciful	some	there
hearty	was	to
illusion	who	too
scenic		whole

1. There have been / many fanciful tales / about cowboys / in the old days.

2. This story / is about a cowgirl / that lived / in the old days, / too.

3. Her name / was Texas Kate, / and she / was a behemoth.

4. When she was born, / Kate was just / a plain, ordinary girl.

5. Later, / it would seem / that she had grown / to a colossal size / very quickly.

6. Texas Kate moved on / to a small scenic town.

7. She cordially asked everyone / if she could have / a hearty meal.

8. Everyone in the town / was very helpful.

9. There are some / who believe / that Texas Kate / was just an illusion.

10. Our town knows / the whole truth!

Name _____

Read the following sentences. Circle the adverb or comparative adverb in each sentence. If there is a double negative, cross out one negative and write a positive word to replace it.

1. Colin and Sarah quickly walked to the van. _____

2. They happily packed their backpacks into the back. _____

3. They eagerly waited for their parents to drive to the campground.

   _____

4. They don't never like to be late to the campsite. _____

5. Sarah's grandparents arrived earlier than anyone else. _____

6. Their grandmother stitched a blanket more beautifully than anyone else.

   _____

7. Colin and Sarah didn't have no tools to set up the tent. _____

8. Their parents could put up the tent more skillfully than Colin and Sarah.

   _____

9. Sarah periodically gave crumbs to the squirrels. _____

10. Colin and Sarah slept most soundly that night. _____

"The Untold Story of Texas Kate"
• **Practice Book**
© Harcourt • Grade 4

Name _____

Writers should organize their ideas in a logical sequence.
When writers are explaining something, a passage is sometimes
organized in a cause-and-effect order.

The paragraph should have a rational beginning, middle, and end.	→	The events can be described using a cause-and-effect organization.	→	The cause-and-effect organization will make the paragraph more understandable.

A. Read the sentences below. Number them to show the correct cause-and-effect order.

_____ Trish fell and scraped her knee.

_____ Trish was running on the playground.

_____ She tripped over a large rock.

B. Read the sentences below. Write them in cause-and-effect order.

1. I slipped in the puddle and got wet.
   It rained hard last night.
   There were puddles of rain this morning.

   _____

   _____

2. I watered the seed.
   I put the seed in the hole.
   I covered the seed with soil.
   I dug a hole in the ground.
   It grew into a pretty flower.

   _____

   _____

   _____

C. Suppose you and a friend had a lemonade stand. On your own paper,
write three sentences in cause-and-effect order that show how you set up and
run your stand.

"The Untold Story of Texas Kate"
• Practice Book

Read the story. Then circle the letter of the correct answer
to each question below.

Mrs. Lopez set the poster board on the chalk ledge. "This poster will show which roles our class has in the fourth-grade musical. It is an hour long and we get to choose two songs to sing." The whole class was excited about the performance. There was a lot of chatter and giggling.

"I want to sing a song about peace around the world," exclaimed Jeff.

"We should sing a familiar song that everyone knows," said Cinda.

"Settle down, everyone. They'll give us a list of songs to choose from. We just have to practice. But first, let's decide on these speaking parts," said Mrs. Lopez. Just as she began to read, a piece of paper slid under the door. "That must be the list of songs," Mrs. Lopez explained.

After she read the paper, Mrs. Lopez's eyes widened and it was plain to see her surprise. "Oh, my," she laughed. "It looks as if Jeff figured out what the play is about. It's called *Peace to the World!*"

1. Why is the whole class excited?
   A Mrs. Lopez mentioned a musical.
   B The students know their parts.
   C Jeff seems to know everything.
   D Mrs. Lopez put up a poster.

2. What do you know about the performance?
   A It is an hour long.
   B No one seems to know his or her part.
   C There are too many songs.
   D The stage will be very plain.

3. What did Jeff want to sing?
   A a song about holes
   B a song about peace
   C a song about pails
   D a song about scents

4. What do they have to do first?
   A sing about peace
   B find a familiar musical piece
   C pick their speaking parts
   D find two songs everyone knows

5. What came under the door?
   A a song about peace
   B a piece of paper
   C two newspapers
   D a list of their names

6. Why was it plain to see that Mrs. Lopez was surprised?
   A Her eyes widened.
   B She turned pale.
   C She was too quiet.
   D She sent away the paper.

"The Untold Story of Texas Kate"
• Practice Book
© Harcourt • Grade 4

Name _____

coddled	been	disagreement
dainty	laugh	disappearance
dedicated	some	incorrectly
determined	their	remarkable
endured	they	unhappily
memorable	two	unusually
pitiful	were	

1. This is a remarkable story / about some sailors / on an expedition / to the South Pole.

2. These sailors knew / that they would not / be coddled.

3. They were determined / to sail through / the unusually thick ice packs.

4. They quickly realized / the pitiful shape / of their ship.

5. Sailors / began to have disagreements / and behaved unhappily.

6. The narrator / told about several memorable events / that took place on the ship / to make sailors laugh again.

7. Even though the wooden ship / was not dainty, / it cracked.

8. The captain / led the sailors / to Elephant Island.

9. The sailors were dedicated / to their captain, / and knew that he / would not steer them incorrectly.

10. Even though the captain's disappearance / had been two years ago, / the sailors endured / and later were rescued.

"Caught in the Ice!" • Practice Book
© Harcourt • Grade 4

Name _____

Rewrite each sentence, adding the correct punctuation.

1. Sissy had to go to the grocery store the bank and the cleaners.

   _____

2. We have to clean up she said.

   _____

3. David read Stuart Little over the holiday break.

   _____

4. Stephanie likes to swim but she forgot to bring her swimsuit.

   _____

5. No I do not want any dessert.

   _____

6. We sang America the Beautiful in our show.

   _____

7. He said I have a blue van.

   _____

Name _____

Writers should organize their ideas in a logical sequence.
Writers use sequence words to make the order of the steps
clear and to tie together the sentences in the paragraph.

Sequence words can help order steps or connect ideas. ➡ Some examples of **sequence words** are *finally, next, after, now, before, when,* and *last.*

A. Read the sentences. Underline the sequence words.

First, we went home. After that, we had a snack.

1. We wanted to go play football next.

2. After we found the ball, we went to the playground.

3. Before we could begin, we had to find enough players.

4. Finally, we were able to play our game.

B. Read the sentences. Circle the sequence words.

   Becky finally got to go to Dena's house after finishing her homework. When she got there, Becky asked, "What do you want to do now?"

C. Imagine that you are telling your friend about something that happened over the weekend. On a separate sheet of paper, write sentences describing the event. Use sequence words to tie your ideas together.

"Caught in the Ice!" • Practice Book
© Harcourt • Grade 4

Name _____

Read the story. Circle all the long words with both prefixes and suffixes.

Jenny tapped impatiently on the table. She was waiting for her sister to finish her homework. She seemed to be unusually slow today. "Come on, Ellen, don't you want to go to the carnival?" Jenny reminded her sister that they had somewhere to go.

"Jenny, don't rush your sister. We have plenty of time," explained their mother.

Jenny didn't want to cause a disagreement, so she went to her room. It was unlikely she could make Ellen hurry. This was going to be her first visit to a carnival. Her friends told her that she would have a remarkable time. They told her about the unhealthy but delicious refreshments. She heard about the fun rides. At night, she knew there would be lights and fireworks, too. Jenny smiled as she thought about the exciting time she was about to have.

Circle and write the word that best completes each sentence.

1. Jenny's sister was _____ slow about finishing her homework.

   impatiently   unusually   remarkable

2. Jenny didn't want to cause a _____, so she went to her room.

   departure   disappearance   disagreement

3. Jenny knew that their night at the carnival was going to be _____.

   remarkable   refreshment   refillable

4. She was very curious about the _____ at the carnival.

   refreshments   disappearance   unhealthy

5. Were the refreshments really _____?

   unusually   unhappily   unhealthy

Name _____

abruptly	been	scene
descend	come	sent
discern	eyes	specific
distinguished	here	to
dubious	very	unusually
estimate		
frantically		
scrutinize		
verify		
vicinity		

1. Carter had been / in this vicinity / for four years / looking for one specific thing.

2. Carter had come here / to find King Tut's chambers.

3. Many scientists felt / that Carter could not finish / this dubious mission.

4. Carter felt that / his very distinguished career / would be over / if he did not find the chambers.

5. Carter made sure / that his unusually fine team of workers / did not run around frantically.

6. Carter stopped his work abruptly / to verify that the water bearer / had found something.

7. After he began / to scrutinize the sand, / his eyes widened.

8. Carter sent a note / to Lord Carnarvon / to tell him about the scene.

9. It was so dark, / they couldn't discern how many steps / they would have to descend.

10. Carter could not estimate / the value of the objects / he found in the chambers.

119

"Beneath the Sands" • Practice Book

Grammar:
Irregular Verbs,
Contractions,
and Possessive
Pronouns
. . . .
Lesson 30

Name _____

**Read each sentence. Circle the correct word and write it in
the blank.**

1. My family _____ to Florida for our summer vacation.

   drived   drive   drove

2. We _____ swim suits and toys for the beach.

   brought   bringed   brings

3. We were so excited to get _____.

   they're   there   their

4. _____ going to the beach today?

   Who's   Whose   Who

5. Jasmine _____ that swim suit before.

   wore   has worn   worn

6. The weather forecast predicts that _____ going to be hot today.

   it's   its   it

7. Dusty _____ go to the festival on Friday night.

   couldn't   coul'dnt   cou'ldnt

8. I have _____ about the beach in my journal.

   wrote   write   written

"Beneath the Sands" • **Practice Book**
© Harcourt • Grade 4

Name _____

Read the following sentences. Circle the adverbs in each sentence. Add the correct punctuation where needed.

1. Cassidy said, I want to read *Tom Sawyer*.

2. She likes to be able to read quietly in her room.

3. I finished the book swiftly, she announced.

4. Cassidy bought a new book yesterday.

5. We sang B-I-N-G-O at school today.

6. Trey read the article In the Water in the newspaper.

7. Tony said, You swim more quickly than I do.

8. "I will happily go with you to the pool" she said.

9. Did you hear All I Really Need on the radio?

10. Yesterday we saw the movie The Treasures of Egypt.

121

"Beneath the Sands" • Practice Book

Circle the letter in front of the sentence that best describes the picture.

1. A Kevin used his binoculars to see the scenery better.

   B Kevin has a knack for photography.

   C Kevin heard a rustling in the bushes.

2. A Kevin sends a telegraph.

   B Kevin instructs his brother on using the binoculars.

   C Kevin is looking for a specific bird.

3. A The bird is unusually quiet.

   B The bird is restoring her nest.

   C The bird is putting worms in containers.

4. A Look at the two eggs.

   B Look at the bird fly to the tree.

   C The bird can sing too.

5. A Kevin constructs his own nest at home.

   B Kevin writes a paragraph about the bird.

   C Kevin inspects the nest.

6. A Kevin was unusually cold.

   B Kevin turned pale when he saw the bird.

   C Kevin got some birdseed out of the pail.

7. A Kevin needs to refill the pail.

   B Kevin sees something remarkable.

   C Kevin impatiently waits for more seeds.

"Beneath the Sands" • Practice Book
© Harcourt • Grade 4